APPALACHIAN HERITAGE

VOL. 43, NO. 1
WINTER 2015

ESTABLISHED IN 1973

PUBLISHED QUARTERLY
by Berea College
CPO 2166
205 N. Main Street
Berea, KY, 40404

www.appalachianheritage.net

 Periodicals postage paid at Berea, Kentucky, and at additional mailing offices. ISSN# 03632318.

Electronic submissions only at www.appalachianheritage.net

Distributed by the University of North Carolina Press. Basic subscription price: $30/year for individuals, $40/year for institutions. For subscription requests and inquiries, visit the magazine's website, email uncpress_journals@unc.edu, or call 919.962.4201.

CONTENTS

EDITOR'S NOTE............*Jason Howard* 5

2014 DENNY C. PLATTNER AWARDS............ 8

FICTION

Broke Your Heart Just About Every Way How ....*Clarissa Nemeth* 10

Still Life in Townsend............*Melanie K. Hutsell* 44

Luck of the Draw............*Elaine Fowler Palencia* 66

Fall............*Adam Padgett* 87

CREATIVE NONFICTION

Picking Tomatoes, Near Freeze, at Midnight ....*Richard Hague* 28

Christmas in August............*Jennifer Barton* 102

POETRY

To Even Be Different to Begin With Tears at Your Skin ....*Savannah Sipple* 26

The Mountain Man Searches for Signs of Change ....*Savannah Sipple* 27

Rural Stigmata............*Jen Coleman* 33

Sunt Lacrimae Rerum............*Amanda Rachelle Warren* 34

The Strip Mine Girl............*Matthew Haughton* 43

Removal Act: John Young Squirrel
.... *William Kelley Woolfitt* 62
Shall Cleave Unto .... *William Kelley Woolfitt* 64
The Poet's House Was a Trip .... *Allison Thorpe* 75
Barren .... *Kathryn Cody* 76
Before Graceland .... *Lauren Albin* 83
Hydrangea Ridge .... *Tina Mozelle Braziel* 84
To Shake Another .... *Tina Mozelle Braziel* 86
Black Dog .... *Cathy Lentes* 100
Viduity from a Rooftop .... *Terrell Jamal Terry* 118
Scythe .... *Terrell Jamal Terry* 120

INTERVIEW
David Joy .... *Jason Howard* 51

CRAFT ESSAY
The Sacred Stillness of Father Damien
.... *Katherine Scott Crawford* 77

SPECIAL FEATURE
Kentucky Writers in Kentucky .... *Wendell Berry* 36

BOOK REVIEWS
Driving with the Dead (Hicks) .... *Erin Keane* 122
Every Leaf a Mirror: A Jim Wayne Miller Reader (Grubbs & Miller) .... *Nicholas Smith* 126

CONTRIBUTORS 132

COVER PHOTOGRAPH
Guiding Light .... *C. Williams*

EDITOR'S NOTE

JASON HOWARD

In the dead of winter, sunlight is often in short supply, appearing without warning, only to soon disappear again behind a mass of grey clouds. Many of us can't help but walk around downcast, wearing what Shakespeare called a "February face" in *Much Ado About Nothing*—"So full of frost, of storm and cloudiness..." We pine for the sun, for warmer temperatures, for woods and beaches and the heat of city sidewalks beneath our sandaled feet.

The writing in this issue will not be a cure-all for those February faces. There are clouds and storms within these pages, moments of sadness and stark beauty that reflect the winter's chill. But tucked away in here are also rays of sunlight. All are gifts from the talented group of writers huddled here who ask you to contemplate a small town tragedy in the story "Broke Your Heart Just About Every Way How" by Clarissa Nemeth, a glimpse behind the veneer of country music legend Dolly Parton in the essay "Christmas in August" by Jennifer Barton, how pain can leave a mark in the poem "Rural Stigmata" by Jen Coleman, and quietude in literature in the craft essay "The Sacred Stillness of Father Damien" by Katherine Scott Crawford.

I'm also proud to announce the winners of the 2014 Denny C. Plattner Awards, presented to the authors of the work deemed by our judges to be the best pieces of fiction, creative nonfiction, and poetry that appeared in the magazine last year.

The fiction award goes to Patti Frye Meredith for her story "The Big Chair." Bestselling novelist and judge Denise Giardina does not mince words, stating, "Meredith's story is carefully crafted, her characters are fully realized and believable, and their lives are ultimately moving." Honorable mention in fiction was awarded to Jordan Farmer for his story "Lost in the Flood."

Fenton Johnson is the recipient of the creative nonfiction award for his essay "Power and Obedience: Restoring Pacifism to American Politics." In his comments, essayist and judge Patrick Madden observes, "By personal, familial, and regional stories with philosophical statements, military history, and the development of the Titan Missile system, Johnson crafts a powerful essay on the pervasiveness of war and the importance of pacifism...His personal experiences and meditations invite readers to ponder their own complicities in systems that seek to destroy rather than heal. 'Power and Obedience: Restoring Pacifism to American Politics' does what the best essays do: it grapples with irremediable complexities through a strong individual voice that stands within the melee and does not flee." Receiving honorable mention in this category is Angel Sands Gunn for her essay "Black Holes."

The poetry award is presented to Maurice Manning for his poem "Translation." Acclaimed poet Kathleen Driskell, who judged this genre, notes, "Upon entering Manning's fine poem, I understood within a line or two that this poem was from a master's hand. There are so many things I could say about it in admiration—beginning with the word 'so' that commences the poem and lets the reader know this is an ongoing conversation the speaker has with self, but also a conversation with his own culture and even poetry (I hear and see habits of haiku throughout). Manning's voice is completely of our present world, even as it effortlessly reaches back and engages the old work of poet as philosopher." Driskell awarded honorable mention to L.S. McKee for her poem "The Creek."

With all that said, I now leave you to the winter—chilly and partly cloudy, but with a strong chance of some sunshine. ■

2014 DENNY C. PLATTNER AWARDS

The annual Plattner Awards were established in 1995 by Kenneth and Elissa Plattner to honor their late son and his love of writing. The awards are given to the finest pieces of fiction, creative nonfiction, and poetry that appeared in *Appalachian Heritage* during the previous year. Winners receive a $200 prize, and both winners and honorable mentions are awarded a handsome cherry wooden book rack designed and manufactured by Berea College Crafts.

FICTION

Judged by Denise Giardina, author of Storming Heaven *and* Saints and Villains

Winner: Patti Frye Meredith, "The Big Chair"
Honorable Mention: Jordan Farmer, "Lost in the Flood"

CREATIVE NONFICTION

Judged by Patrick Madden, author of Quotidiana

Winner: Fenton Johnson, "Power and Obedience: Restoring Pacifism to American Politics"
Honorable Mention: Angel Sands Gunn, "Black Holes"

POETRY

Judged by Kathleen Driskell, author of Seed Across Snow *and* Laughing Sickness

Winner: Maurice Manning, "Translation"
Honorable Mention: L.S. McKee, "The Creek"

BROKE
YOUR HEART JUST ABOUT EVERY WAY HOW

CLARISSA NEMETH

Her baby son, Jett, three-years-old and fighting a nasty cold, slept next to Brenda in her bed. She sat rigid with her back to the headboard and her knees pulled tight to her chest beneath the ragged blanket, listening to his every sniffle and wet breath. She reached over to his thick brown curls and hovered her hand over the place where they swirled just above his left temple, the place where the other boy's head had been sticky and matted with blood. That boy had blonde hair, finer than Jett's, with a cowlick at the crown. She couldn't bring herself to touch the spot. She was due back at the Pump Stop at seven. Dale had offered her the day shift for the next few weeks. It was kind of him, but she hadn't slept more than a few hours that night or the one before, startling awake several times to strangle her churning dreams.

Out in the hallway she heard footsteps and then the flush of the toilet. Momma was up. Brenda stayed perfectly still and tried to match her breaths exactly to Jett's while grey light crept in through the blinds. His lungs filled up so much faster than hers did. When she smelled bacon she eased herself out of the bed, careful not to wake Jett, and wrapped herself in her frayed cotton robe.

Momma shuffled around the kitchen, fussing with the coffee maker and taking the occasional hit from her inhaler. She set out another mug for Brenda and said, "That mess is in the paper again this morning."

"Still?"

Momma nodded at the pages of the Caller scattered on the countertop. "Front page."

Brenda found the headline beneath a story about the state university firing its basketball coach. Jamestown Shootings Determined to be Murder-Suicide. She scanned it until she found the one piece of information she needed; she knew the rest of it well enough.

"Cody Williams," Brenda murmured.

As if it had been a question, Momma replied, "Nothing like that ever happened when I was growing up. We was raised with Christian values. You take God out the schools and now you got mommas shooting their babies in the head." She gave Brenda a plate of bacon and toast. "Here."

Brenda's head throbbed. "Momma, I don't think that's really it."

"You don't know a thing about it, Brenda. Just last year they tried to stop the prayer before the football games in Shelby County. No one gets raised with respect for God anymore, and you seen with your own eyes what comes of it." Momma nodded towards the paper again.

Brenda nibbled at the toast. It was true enough she didn't know anything about the world—she hadn't even finished high school—but she was pretty sure praying before football games didn't have a thing to do with the scene in the Pump Stop bathroom Sunday night. The seconds on the microwave clicked by, one after another, until Momma asked, "You gonna eat your bacon?"

The sight of the glistening red meat, streaked with fat, turned her stomach. "I have to shower. You eat it." She drained her coffee and wiped her mouth.

"You better wake Jett for breakfast."

Brenda paused in the doorway to the kitchen. "He's still sick, Momma. Let him sleep. You can wake him after I leave."

■ ■ ■

She'd been working at the Pump Stop for over a year now, and it wasn't too bad. Dale Kemp was good to her and flexible about her shifts. On that Sunday night he'd come straight from home, still in sweatpants, and he had cried when he saw the bathroom. Brenda had never seen a man cry before. Dale was a deacon over at Banner Springs Baptist and he said a prayer over the boy before they loaded him up in the ambulance. Brenda thought he would do one over the mother, too, but he didn't. She guessed she understood why.

Brenda never thought much about work like other people seemed to, never complained about it like her husband Zeb used to before he ran off. Work was just something she had to do, like grocery shopping or brushing her teeth: tedious, but nothing to dread. She liked it better than she'd liked high school, where she always had to worry about what she wore and what she said and who she said it to. Work was so much easier. She wore the uniform; she smiled at people and rang up the register so it told her how much change; she turned on the pumps and told everyone to have a nice day. The Pump Stop wasn't even that busy, especially since Dale had put her on the night shift. At home she never had much quiet time, and it was nice to spend the hours daydreaming, listening to the country music piped over the speakers and watching the hot dog carousel spin round and round and round.

This was the first morning she'd ever felt bad pulling into the station. She felt like she might throw up, and her hands shook when she lit her first cigarette of the day. Dale's truck was in his usual spot and she didn't want to look like a mess in front of him. He might send her home for another day and that would be even worse.

She liked it better than she'd liked high school, where she always had to worry about what she wore and what she said and who she said it to.

Running her eyes over the scratched tile floor, the rows of snack food, the coolers full of drinks, for the first time in her life she was amazed at a place for looking the same way it always had. Behind the counter, Dale, in his checkered shirt and Vols cap, looked exactly like he always did. She had the quick thought that she, too, must look unchanged, before he said, "Good morning, Brenda. How you doing today?"

"Fine."

He nodded. "Good, good. You seen the paper this morning?"

"Yessir."

"I already had some people ask about it. I'd appreciate it if you didn't go talking about it. We ought to just put the whole thing behind us. You just say it's a real tragedy and we're all praying for that family."

"Sure thing."

He patted her on the shoulder. "You ever need to pray with me, you just tell me, alright?"

"Thanks, Dale. I'm really okay."

He shook his head. "The Lord just works in strange ways sometimes, don't he?"

Brenda shrugged. She didn't feel like she knew very much about the Lord's ways. She'd gone to Sunday school for her entire childhood, but fat Mrs. Meeks with her old lady smell and dirty glasses never once talked about any of the problems she'd ever faced since, like what to do if your husband got tired of you and then just up and left, or if your father died owing the bank a lot of money, or how to get blood off your best pair of blue jeans. There would be no purpose saying any of this to Dale, either, not a word.

More people than usual came into the Pump Stop that morning. Folks were curious. Some made offhand comments at the register, leaning over like they were telling her a secret: "I heard about that awful mess on Sunday. What a shame." Brenda thought it was strange that so many people referred to it that way, like it was just a bunch of spilled milk over in the dairy section. But of course, it had made a mess; that was true enough.

It was all more or less alright until Sean Kilby came in to buy a pack of Camels while Dale was out on lunch break. Brenda had gone to high school with Sean; back then, he'd been lazy and mean. Now everyone said he sold meth out of his trailer over by the city park. He came right up to her at the counter and said, "Was you the one worked Sunday night?"

"I'd rather not say, Sean."

"Aw, come on. Most interesting thing ever happened in Jamestown and you won't tell me one little bit about it?"

"It was a tragedy. I'm praying for the family." She slid him his pack of cigarettes. "That'll be five dollars sixteen."

"Sure, sure." He leaned with one elbow on the counter and reached back to pull out his wallet. He smelled like sweat and dirt, and the way he rolled an old toothpick around with his tongue made her want to slap it out of his mouth.

"Woman must've been right out her mind," Sean continued. "She look crazy when she came in?"

"How am I supposed to know?"

"You know, like—" he widened his red eyes and rolled them around in gross parody. "Like she was on something."

Brenda handed him the change.

"She say anything? Did the kid say anything?"

"When did you make detective, Sean? I didn't know the sheriff's department was hiring meth cooks."

Sean sucked at the toothpick in his mouth. Then he said, "You got a little boy about that same age, don't you, Brenda?"

She looked down at the countertop and counted her breaths in the silence until he backed away, whistling. She looked up when she heard the electronic chime of the open door, just in time to see him spit the toothpick out onto the floor behind him.

■ ■ ■

When the girl and her son had come in beneath that same chime, there had been nothing out of the ordinary. The police had asked Brenda, and she had asked herself a dozen times, whether there had been any hint of trouble, but there truly had been nothing. That bothered her. She wanted to believe that somehow she'd be able to sense something bad coming in, that her body would know ever if her mind couldn't—that at least the hair on the back of her neck would stand up. But on that warm March night when they come in she'd been thinking about how Jett's feet were getting bigger and he needed a new pair of shoes.

The mother had frizzy brown hair and wore a puffy, oversize hunting jacket over sweatpants. Brenda had said hello, but the girl ignored her and headed straight to the back of the store towards the red sign that said RESTROOMS. The little boy had on a dinosaur T-shirt and he stared up at that blue Slushee machine until his momma came back and took him by the hand to lead him with her, walking so fast she was pulling him and his sneakers squeaked against the floor.

The summer Brenda turned ten, the kids in her grade were finally allowed to jump off the big diving board at the community center pool, and they took turns daring each other, saying "scaredy-cat" and "chicken" to anyone who hesitated. Brenda was terrified of heights but when they dared her she knew she had to do it. She made herself walk very fast up that ladder and jump the very moment she got to the edge, because she knew that if she hesitated, even just for a second, she wouldn't be able to do it.

The way that girl had walked into the bathroom at the Pump Stop was the same way Brenda had walked to the diving board that muggy summer afternoon years before. But by the time Brenda realized that, it was too late for her to do anything but call Dale and the police.

■ ■ ■

Just before Brenda finished the shift, Amy Lorch, another old classmate of hers, came in to pay for a tank of gas. She made a beeline for Brenda and slapped both of her palms on the countertop. "Brenda! I couldn't wait to get over here to talk to you. I just can't believe that girl was Laurie Williams. When I saw it in the paper this morning I just thought, *wowee, who'd think a person I knew would grow up and be a murderer?*"

"You knew her?"

"Well, I didn't, like, know her. She went to school over at Cobbville. But when she was little her parents went to our church for a few years, and my mom said they were good people. She said they must just be beside themselves that Laurie would do such a terrible thing. Mom doesn't understand why Laurie didn't just leave the boy with her parents, since they were the ones raising him anyway. I guess they would have—Laurie can't have been much good for a mother."

"When I saw it in the paper this morning I just thought, wowee, who'd think a person I knew would grow up and be a murderer?"

"Where do they live?"

"Who?"

"Laurie's parents."

"Way out the pike, almost in Shelby County. You know where the old First Methodist Church was before we moved closer to town? That's when her parents stopped going and they live on that road right down past the cemetery. I heard Laurie was no good after she got knocked up but no one ever thought she'd do anything like what she did on Sunday. I mean, I just can't believe it." Amy shook her head. "We used to play tag in the field out there by the church. Then she grows up and murders her own baby."

"It's a tragedy. I'm praying for them."

Amy raised an eyebrow. "I'm praying for that little angel baby, but not for her, I'll tell you that much." She cast her eyes back towards the bathrooms. "They clean up all that mess back there?"

Brenda blinked. "Dale had somebody come in. I don't know much about it."

Amy leaned in closer and lowered her voice. "You think I could go back and take a look?"

■ ■ ■

Brenda didn't realize she was going to pass the turn to her house until she was doing it. She kept driving down the main drag of Jamestown, out past the high school. Rain fell in limp, uneven bursts, spattering the windshield and drifting down in sheets on the eaves of the squat brick buildings and the aluminum bleachers under which she and Zeb had squirreled themselves to go all the way. She drove on, past the rippling brown hills and patchwork farmsteads that dotted the landscape. Past the tractor supply and the dilapidated, nameless strip club where she'd considered working before Dale came through with the Pump Stop job. The cars she passed numbered fewer and fewer and the road narrowed when she rounded the curve to face the old church. Vandals had shattered the windows long ago, and only half of them were covered with plywood. The holes looked like empty eye sockets, the orange spray of graffiti on the door like a howling mouth.

The first house past the cemetery was an old trailer sitting unevenly atop its concrete blocks, but it had a little garden and the yard was free of old cars and junk. The black metal mailbox said WILLIAMS in white reflective letters, and even as Brenda pulled her car up the gravel drive she wasn't sure why she was doing it.

A fine mist of rain settled over her hair while she waited on the concrete stoop, hugging her arms to her chest in the cold. She heard the yipping of a small dog before the door opened. A little dirty-white terrier jumped and pawed at the screen on its hind legs. Behind it stood a heavyset woman in a thin blue housecoat. Her hair was loose and grey, and she had handkerchief balled in one hand.

"Who are you?" the woman asked. "What do you want?"

Brenda had to clear her throat before she could speak. "My name is Brenda Lackey, ma'am. I didn't mean to bother you, I just..." she trailed off.

On and on the dog barked. "Are you from the paper? We don't want to talk to no one from the paper."

"No, ma'am, I—I only just wanted to say how sorry I am. I was the one working that night. At the station. When Laurie..." Brenda swallowed. "I was the one working."

The woman bent over and in one motion grabbed the dog's collar and swept it aside. The screen door squeaked on its hinges when she held it open. "Come in."

The interior was dark and smelled of pot roast and dog hair. Wiping her feet, Brenda made out the figure of a man sitting in an overstuffed chair. An oxygen tank was parked next to it and its tubing ran up the arm of the chair. The dog ran in circles around the room, barking, and the woman snapped, "Mitzi!" to no apparent effect. From the chair, the man yelled, "Who's that?"

Mrs. Williams settled herself on the couch without offering Brenda anything. Unsure whether to sit, Brenda stood awkwardly by the door, toeing the dog away with her shoe.

"This girl was with Cody," Mrs. Williams said.

"What?"

"I SAID THIS GIRL WAS WITH CODY. AT THE GAS STATION."

"What was she there for?"

"SHE WAS WORKING."

"Oh."

Mrs. Williams patted the spot on the couch next to her. "Come sit." Brenda eased her way over and sat on the edge of the couch beside her. Mrs. Williams reached over to a side table,

The picture had been taken in summer. His hair was sun-bleached and his feet were bare and he lay belly down in a swing...

picked up a photograph in a plastic frame, and handed it to Brenda. "This was our Cody," she said.

The picture had been taken in summer. His hair was sun-bleached and his feet were bare and he lay belly down in a swing, his hands gripping the rusty chain, his legs flared out behind him. "He's beautiful," Brenda said.

"I want you to see that precious boy so when you think of him, you don't think of what you saw then." Mrs. Williams dabbed at her eyes with the handkerchief. "He was our angel. I know Jesus was there take his hand."

"I'm so sorry."

"Don't you be sorry. Wasn't you that took his life away."

Brenda didn't know what to say. The dog had retired to a corner and the only sound now was the hiss of the old man's oxygen tubing. Mrs. Williams handed her another picture. Brenda recognized the slate grey background from her own years of school pictures. "That was from her last year of high school, when she was sixteen."

Laurie Williams, only four years earlier, had a youthful chubbiness in her cheeks that Brenda couldn't recall on the gaunt girl from the Pump Stop bathroom. Brenda knew well how having a baby could melt such things away and replace them with bruised eyes and lank hair.

"I have prayed," Mrs. Williams said. "I have prayed and prayed, and I just don't understand it. Laurie never did find her way. Never did do well in school, never made a right choice over wrong, never thought of no one but her own self. She got into trouble left and right. Drove off that sweet baby's father, ran him all the way to Kentucky. She promised me she didn't need him! Well, and no surprise, with us here to do all the work. But I believed her the other night when she said she was going out to get Cody an Icee. She took her daddy's old pistol and I didn't know. I thought they was going out for Icees."

"Cody loved a treat," Mr. Williams wheezed.

"Yes, he did. He did. And Laurie knew it." Mrs. Williams closed her eyes.

"I'm so sorry," Brenda said again.

Mrs. Williams was crying now. "Did she say even a word to you?"

"No, ma'am. I'm sorry, but she didn't."

"I just don't understand. Why would she do such a thing? Why?"

"The Lord works in strange ways," her husband said from his chair.

The words stirred Brenda to standing. She realized two things at once—that she had come here with the hope of telling them something, and that she could not, after all, tell them. "I should go," she said. "I don't want to bother y'all anymore. I just wanted to tell you—how sorry I am."

"You have children?" boomed Mr. Williams.

"No, sir," she lied. "I have to get on home, my momma's waiting up for me."

"You're a good girl," Mrs. Williams said, rising to show her out. "You take care of your momma. Laurie never did give us respect. She broke your heart just every way how." She seized Brenda's hand, cupping it between her own, cold and moist. "We are having a service for Cody over at Savior Methodist in Cobbville on Saturday. We sure would love it if you came."

"Oh, of course."

"It was a real blessing for you to come," Mrs. Williams continued. "We are so glad you could be with our Cody at the end. So he wasn't alone."

The rain was coming down harder, and as Brenda ran through the mud to the car she could hear the barking of the little terrier and the high voice pleading, "Mitzi!" They echoed in her head long after she had pulled out of the driveway and left them behind.

■ ■ ■

When she got home Momma was in the living room, smoking and watching the television. "You're late," her mother chided her. "Jett done went to bed."

Brenda hung up her coat and began to clean up the dishes in the kitchen. "Was he feeling any better?"

"Not hardly. His fever's up again and he didn't want dinner. He asked after you. I didn't know what to tell him."

"I'm sorry I was late." Brenda paused. Could she tell her mother? "I went out to see the parents of that girl to pay my respects."

"No respect due, you ask me," Momma said. "Can't be much for parents if they reared a daughter like that."

"You raised me. I got pregnant young, same as she did."

Momma stabbed her cigarette out in the ashtray. "I won't hear you blame me for that. You made that bed yourself and you been lying in it ever since. I wasn't the one went out all gussied up like a tramp. I wasn't the one spreading my legs for that no-good Zeb Carter."

"You were the one that made me marry him. You were the one that made me have his baby."

Momma gasped. "I never heard a girl blame so much on her mother. Your daddy would beat you black and blue for that, and you know it. We done nothing but take care of you since the day you were born."

Brenda closed her eyes, suddenly weary of the argument, and the righteous anger she'd felt searing her moments ago evaporated. "Alright," she said. "Let's not yell, I don't want to wake Jett."

"What on earth has gotten into you?"

"I'm tired, Momma." She gazed up at the ceiling, the blue-black ring of mold around the kitchen light. "I'm just tired."

■ ■ ■

In the middle of the night Jett's coughing woke her from a fitful sleep. Each breath he drew sent him into spasms of wet barking. "Oh, buddy," she said, rubbing his back, "what are we going to do for you?"

She ran the shower as hot as it could go until clouds of steam floated out when she opened the bathroom door. She sat at the edge of the tub with Jett, rocking him against her chest in a towel, humming whatever melodies she could recall from her childhood.

She stared at the cracked tile of the bathroom floor in a stupor brought on by heat, exhaustion, and worry. Through the swirl of the steam rose the memory of that last glimpse of Laurie Williams leading her little boy into the ladies' room. The steel hot dog basket making one turn. And then the gunshots.

At first she thought a car had backfired, but there was only one car in the lot. She ran to the bathrooms, thinking surely they couldn't have been gunshots, and yet with each step more certain they were. When she reached the door she hesitated, only for a moment, thinking about the boy's hand in his mother's.

There was so much blood, much more than Brenda even expected. The boy had fallen with his head slumped against the dirty white wall beneath the paper towel dispenser. The mother lay face up, her feet beneath the sink, and Brenda let out a strangled cry because the woman was looking at her, still alive, though the devastation of her face would surface each night in Brenda's dreams.

She ran the shower as hot as it could go until clouds of steam floated out when she opened the bathroom door.

The woman made a strange, helpless noise. Brenda steadied herself with one hand against the wall. "I'll call 911. It's okay, I'm gonna go call right now."

The woman made another keening sound and lifted a trembling hand to point to the boy.

And though Brenda could not have said how, she understood what the woman wanted.

Brenda got down on her hands and knees in the blood and leaned over beneath the paper towel dispenser to place two fingers on the boy's neck, brought her cheek down to his face. She met the gaze of the dying woman.

"He's dead. Alright? You did it. He's gone."

And as Brenda stumbled to her feet and ran to get the phone, she heard that woman, who had muddled her own death so badly, weeping, and Brenda understood that weeping as a kind of relief.

She made the call and then came back to the bathroom. The woman's breathing was rasping and uneven. She was looking at her son. The fluorescent bathroom light flickered above the scene, and Brenda listened but heard no sirens, and still the woman stared at her son.

Brenda knelt again in the blood and held her hand.

By the time the paramedics arrived, she was dead.

Jett coughed again. The wet air was starting to work, because Brenda felt a warm slime of mucous run down her chest. She wiped it away with the edge of the towel.

"Momma," he said, "I wanna milkshape."

"We don't have any ice cream, baby," she said absently.

"But I want it," he whined.

The bathroom mirror was fogged over, and where she would have seen her tired reflection and Jett's red face staring back, Brenda saw only their most indistinct shapes. It was as if the two of them were barely there. Brenda's throat tightened. She smoothed Jett's damp brow, trying to murmur something comforting, but whatever words she might have said were gone, stolen away, drifting towards the ceiling in a cloud of steam. ■

TO EVEN BE DIFFERENT TO BEGIN WITH TEARS AT YOUR SKIN

like walking through briars every day,
every minute. It slams you into lockers,

calls you names, follows you down the hall,
cat calls from across the street, whispers

as you walk by, head facing ground. It grinds you
down, sharpens you, like a pencil, stains you

like grease, like oil from a car. It leaves tracks
on your skin. It makes you fear your own bones,

afraid to be yourself, afraid you might break,
or get broken, cracked like when an egg hits pavement.

It makes you change or hide the way you wave,
or stand, or speak, and what you say because one

grin, one glance, might give you away. It shouldn't
leave you awake at night to wonder, but it does.

It shouldn't ache this much to live.

SAVANNAH SIPPLE

THE MOUNTAIN MAN SEARCHES FOR SIGNS OF CHANGE

So may the sun rise, bring hope where it once was forgotten.
—*"Upward Over the Mountain" by Iron & Wine*

I rise early in March, weather flirting
with warmth, sit by the pond, coffee in hand, whiskey
in my pocket, toes in wet grass.
I have to believe life is about these moments:

the slopping sound water makes as wind rubs its back,
the rising sun in my eyes that draws me
to the edge of the pond, into the woods.
It's around this time of year I realize

I have years left to work the mines, in the dark,
away from grass still asleep from winter, breezes strumming
through trees. I am sad beauty can be ripped out, blown apart,
and buried beneath the rubble, like I could be.

The whiskey is the weight of waiting, of not knowing,
of wondering if knowing would make me any different.

SAVANNAH SIPPLE

PICKING
TOMATOES, NEAR FREEZE, AT MIDNIGHT

RICHARD HAGUE

Almost twenty years ago now, one summer's night, I led a party of the blind—myself included—into a deep woods full of copperheads and barbed wire. Scruffy partisans of the sixties all, we had sat on the porch of my trailer in the woods of southeastern Ohio drinking beer until the sky clouded over with the beginnings of a storm, and the moon fled the hollow and pulled the black hat over its face. We'd run out of lies and quasi-autobiographical exaggerations and had reworked to triteness our chronicles of protest and violence and flight. The dog had descended into an immobile sleep under the trailer, and the barred owl, usually loud down Foreaker, roosted in mute stupor. As for us, drinking and drinking, the world seemed to careen and swerve, as if to spin us off it like the mud off a tire.

We had to reassert our verticality, our uprightness in the face of all that leveling. So up we stood, and into the world we went, over the Russian-olived hill, past the Chinese chestnuts and the wind-ruined outhouse that lay like the wreckage of a longboat among the pitch pines. The going was easy at first; I was so familiar with the way that I could have navigated the initial fifty yards in my sleep. But twenty yards more and the path died out like a sentence with no verb. It evaporated, went away, and what brooded in the darkness before us was a tangle of burdock and tickweed and greenbrier strangling an old fence line, then a deep glade of white pines, planted as closely as fence posts, their lowest branches bristling with needles and broken ends.

"Why are we doing this?" someone behind me said.

"Because," I said, "We got to find us some dark."

Earlier, before the clouds had moved in, and while the beer still hummed happily in us, we'd sat with our adam's apples pointed straight up, and ogled the Milky Way. In that good dark dark, ten and more miles from anything even approaching a small town, we could see into the heart of our galaxy, spread like a faint silver eddy in the river of sky above us. We'd fed our eyes, gorged on that looking. But now, in the woods, it was time for the contrast, the absence by which rightly to judge the light.

That's what I thought, anyway. What the others thought, I had no idea. There we were, stumbling into our dread, disobeying one of the most fundamental primate instincts: never go around in the dark.

The guy immediately behind me (there were four of us, a shabby resurrection of pilgrims) suddenly fell. I heard his startled curse and growl. I froze. But then, realizing he'd not been haunch-swiped by a bear the size of a school bus, I relaxed.

Deeper into the dark we staggered, whipped across our eyes by pine branches, tripped by briers and roots. My boot laces came undone; my hat, knocked wopperjawed and off by the flailing arm of another fellow stumbling behind me, flapped away down the gully. Someone started to hum nervously. A whippoorwill exploded from the lee of a windfall ahead of me, and near swooning with surprise, I saw stars. On we pressed.

"Pointless," one said later, back on the trailer porch. We all shivered. We'd broken out every blanket we could find and

Deeper into the dark we staggered, whipped across our eyes by pine branchces, tripped by briers and roots.

sat wrapped like whipped braves in dark's tepee, mumbling bachelors gritty and smoky and pathetic at three in the beery morning.

We'd stood at the far end of the ridge, relatively unscathed, a quarter of a mile back in the woods, and we'd stared out over a blankness that fell off into more of the same. The cloud cover was so thick, and the fog so heavy, that we couldn't see the glow at the ends of our own cigarettes. We'd gotten some dark, all right. Lots of dark. A couple of years' worth of dark. Cheap thrills in the country, the only cost a crazy after-midnight amble.

And that, more or less, is the end of that story.

■ ■ ■

Tonight, a divorce and remarriage and a pair of sons and a hundred poems and three gardens and an old house full of sweat and projects and two steps slower later, I sit in a kitchen flooded with light, two hundred fifty miles from those woods. The oven's still warm from the baking my wife did after supper. Upstairs, the boys sleep wrapped in blankets as the floor registers exhale a desert-dry air and frost ferns unfurl on the glass of their bedroom windows. All is ordered, calm, domestic.

And it's midnight. The weather report in this evening's paper warns of freeze. I fold the pages on the table before me and rustle up my jacket and go out. Overhead, a good clutch of city stars, bright enough to compete with the malls and streetlights: Mizar and its twin in the handle of the Dipper, the clean angles of Orion—Bear and Hunter. The house blocks out the streetlight, and I grub around in the garden beside the driveway, where the light from the kitchen window sprawls spread-eagled on the furrows. I'm fumbling in the cold for the last tomatoes. I'll pick them all, though they're hard and green, and I'll wrap them in pieces of the weather report, the stock market quotations, the local news of teachers and burglars and births. I'll set them on the ledge of the basement wall, and for a couple of weeks, I'll fetch one a day out of the cool dimness into the kitchen light and unwrap a belated surprise—a remnant of high summer in November, a red birth, perhaps, a vegetable Christmas, wrapped in dark but ripening nevertheless.

■ ■ ■

And I am still walking in the dark. For all the changes in my life since that night in the woods long ago, many things inside me—and outside me—have remained the same: hunger for the small deep risks that knowing the world and its mystery require; a crazy attraction to the underbelly of things, to the vagrant and homeless demonstrations of the dark; a wanderlust for the sites of wildnesses and disorders and the odd beauties they often unfold; nostalgia—a real nostalgia, nostalgie de boie—a homesickness for the woods. I do not complain here, or regret. But I know that life is not a matter of deliberations only, despite the truth of Thoreau's work during his sojourn in the woods. More than we commonly acknowledge, life is an accommodation to the unknown and the random, to luck—both good and bad. The dark I sought with my friends back then was not the dark of oblivion, but a dark which like tonight's, holds within it the green hard fruits of potential, fruits that will grow ready and redden, like blood. "Wife, house, children"—but not, as the film version of *Zorba the Greek* finishes, "the full catastrophe."

No. The shape my life has taken is as correct as the shape an oak leaf takes. It is an inheritance, a bequeathal. It is an obligation, an earnest occupation, a duty. And there are rewards for accepting and assuming the shape of a life. The oak leaf flourishes, loyal to its inheritance always, down through the generations fulfilling its obligations to form and function and duty. And it is beautiful for all that.

So too my fumbling in the dark rows this cold night. It is part of my life's shape, my duty. May I continue to place myself here and in all places like it, homing, feeling out the way, moving about in the garden. And if my luck is good, there will be the warmth of a house to return to, the living room golden with light, the air of it filled with the rich measures of Bach, that baker's dozen's daddy, that bright man domestic but untamed. There will be my wife, and our books, and the goldfish on the shelf. And there will be sleep, and day again, and the laughter of our boys. ■

RURAL STIGMATA

I've nurtured the glowing wound:
peroxide, salve,
bandages. I've done right
by this one. The rawness eased,
was replaced
by budding infant
cells. Trenches formed
in the nickel-sized spot
where my fate and life lines
intersected the injury,
two deep vertical red
canals in a waxy purple-pink
circle: a burnt pig's nose,
some grotesque
electrical outlet, the mark
of blaze to come.

JEN COLEMAN

SUNT LACRIMAE RERUM

Sunt lacrimae rerum et mentem mortalia tangent.
(There are tears for things and mortal things touch my mind.) —Virgil

Question the details:

That perfect cylinder of muscle buried in the crook of your knee
and the amen kiss that brands it.

The number of crows in the trees above the field where we were born.

The smell in the breeze:
were it smoke
were it sweet dust in the wake of fell leaves
were it crooked stems broke green beneath them boots
were it the last of the clover
were it metal
                    breath
                                    Sweet William.

Your hair a nothing color till the sun struck it.

Sun raking the tall grass in strange shadows.

That no-name illness heavy lay
and beneath that
                        sorghum-sweet

something twisting tighter
and tighter
and tighter.

AMANDA RACHELLE WARREN

KENTUCKY
WRITERS IN KENTUCKY

WENDELL BERRY

On December 2, 2014, Carnegie Center Director Neil Chethik and Literary Liaison Bianca Spriggs paid a visit to Wendell Berry at his farm in Port Royal, Kentucky. The occasion was Berry's selection as the first living writer to be inducted into the Kentucky Writers Hall of Fame, which is run by the Carnegie Center in Lexington. Tanya Berry,

Wendell's wife of fifty-eight years, invited Chethik and Spriggs inside, where they admired the Berry library while waiting for Wendell to arrive from his writing camp nearby. Then, over tea, a conversation ensued among the four of them about Kentucky writers: *Why are there so many good ones? What are their typical characteristics? What impact do they have on Kentucky politics?* After a few minutes, Wendell took out a small notebook from his shirt pocket and began to jot down notes. The resulting remarks, published below, were delivered to a crowd of more than 400 people at the Carnegie Center on January 28, 2015, as part of the third annual Kentucky Writers Hall of Fame induction ceremony.[1]

■ ■ ■

In the spring of 1964, Tanya and I and our children had been living in New York for two years. When my work in the city ended that spring, we loaded ourselves and our belongings into a Volkswagen Beetle with a luggage rack on top and took the New Jersey Turnpike south. We were returning to Kentucky—to settle, as it turned out, permanently in my home country in Henry County. On my part, this homecoming cost a good deal of worry. Just about every one of my literary friends had told me that I was ruining myself, and I was unable entirely to disbelieve them. Why would a young writer leave a good job in New York, where all the best artistic life and talent had gathered, to go to Kentucky?

There are no "control plots" in a person's life. I have no proof that I would not have done better to stay in New York. But I see that in retrospect my story has gained the brightening of a certain comedy. When I turned my back supposedly on the best of artistic life and talent in New York and came to Kentucky, half believing in my predicted ruin, who was here? Well, among many dear and indispensable others: James Still, Harlan Hubbard, Harry Caudill, Guy Davenport, and Gene Meatyard. All of them I came to know and, I hope, to be influenced by. In 1964 also Thomas Merton was living in Kentucky. I can't say that I knew him as I knew the others, but I had read *The Sign of Jonas* when it was published in 1953, Tanya and I by courtesy of Gene Meatyard visited Merton twice at Gethsemani, and to live here was to feel his presence and his influence. I met Harriette Arnow in, I think, 1955 when I first encountered Mr. Still, at the only writers' conference I ever attended. Many years later I met her again, spoke to her and shook her hand, remembering from then on her eyes and the testing look she gave me. No book more confirms my native agrarianism than *The Dollmaker.*

My point is that in 1964, for a young writer in Kentucky and in need of sustenance, sustenance was here. In the fifty years that have followed, the gathering in Kentucky of Kentucky writers has grown much larger. It would take me a while just to call their names: old friends, allies, influences, members, permitting me to be a member, of an unending, enlightening, entertaining, comforting, indispensable conversation. My further point is that in 2015, for an old writer in Kentucky and in need of sustenance, sustenance is here.

■ ■ ■

Of literary or writerly life in Kentucky I have no worries. It seems lively, various, and dispersed enough to continue, which is all I can presume to ask.

My worries begin when I think of the literary life of Kentucky in the context of the state of Kentucky: a commonwealth enriched by a diversity of regions, but gravely and lastingly fragmented by divisions that are economic, social, cultural, and institutional. These divisions have given us a burdening history of abuse—of land abuse but also and inevitably of the abuse of people, for people and land cannot be destroyed or conserved except together. We all know our history of social and cultural division, from the Indian wars of the eighteenth century to legal discrimination against homosexuals in the twenty-first. And we know how our many divisions, beginning in the lives of persons, become fixed in public and institutional life.

Some public entities that ought to be divided are tightly meshed together. I mean, above all, the intimacy between state government and wealthy industries. Otherwise, the state's institutions and organizations appear to be islands divided, and often in themselves further divided, by specialties, departments, interests, and sides. Where and when might one find a political-industrial-academic-conservationist dialogue on any issue of land use? When aggrieved citizens gather on the pavement in front of the Capitol to express their grievances, who knows it? Who listens? Who replies?

So far as I can tell, those are rhetorical questions, useless except to suggest the extent and seriousness of the fragmentation of our commonwealth. This fragmentation is made possible, and continually made worse, by a cloud of silence that hovers over us. We have in this state no instituted public dialogue, no forum in which a public dialogue could take place.

This public silence ought to be a worry especially to writers. What is the effect or fate, Kentucky writers may ask, of Kentucky books devoted to urgent public issues—*Night Comes to the Cumberlands* or *Lost Mountain* or *Missing Mountains* or *The Embattled Wilderness*? That is not quite a rhetorical question, but the answer is not obvious or easy.

Kentucky writers write books of several kinds, and they publish them, sometimes in Kentucky, but none of their books contributes to a public conversation in Kentucky about books or anything else—in spite of our need for it, and in spite of the schools and other institutions that would benefit from it and could also contribute to it.

We have, besides several private presses, the University Press of Kentucky, which publishes sixty books every year, many of them of interest or concern specifically to Kentuckians. According to Steve Wrinn, editor of the Press, "many" of these books are bought, read, and appreciated by the people of Kentucky. And yet of those books, very few will be reviewed here. The *Courier-Journal,* to name one case in point, is suffering near-fatal typophobia , and publishes no book reviews not piped in from *USA Today.*

Writers now, as never before, must keep aware that literacy is their trade, until now a trade of supreme importance.

And so we can say that we have in Kentucky a sufficiency at least of writers of books, publishers of books, and readers of books. And yet when a Kentucky book is published it enters into a public silence, similar of course to such silences in other states, but in origin and character peculiarly our own. This is a problem that relates immediately to the hope for a sustainable and sustaining human culture in Kentucky. Such a culture, which we must hope for and work for, will depend and thrive upon our diversity of regions, and upon conversation among them. In my long conversation with Gurney Norman, he and I have often spoken as from opposite ends of the Kentucky River watershed. My long conversation with Ed McClanahan has gone back and forth across the hump of northern Kentucky, from two different countries. For me, these dialogues of friendship transcending regional differences have been indispensable sources of instruction and delight. I can't imagine myself without them. Kentucky writers who see their placement here as a shared opportunity and a shared burden may still shape among themselves sustaining friendships and alliances. I hope they do.

■ ■ ■

These are thoughts that have come to me as a writer in Kentucky, in the United States, in the middle of the second decade of the twenty-first century, perhaps at the end of the age of literacy. What might be the use of the role of writers in such a place in such a time? I will say that writers now, as never before, must keep aware that literacy is their trade, until now a trade of supreme importance. Much that we now have that is of greatest value has come to us from books. Our Constitution and Bill of Rights—just to hint at an immeasurable abundance—have come to us from books and from readers of books. To keep our heritage viable and transmissible will require capable writers of books, capable readers of books, and a capable culture of literacy, however small it may have to be.

The survival of literacy in an age of illiteracy may require us to remember how physical, how much of the senses, the life of literacy is. By putting down letters in substantial ink onto a substantial surface for many centuries, we have been making words and then sentences. Putting down the letters, we have felt in our fingers and hands and forearms their shapes and the shapes of the words they make and their flowing together into sentences. We have watched as our hands have done this. We have read by seeing what we have written. As we have written, we have been hearing, at least in our minds, the sounds of our words and sentences. We have been making what Ivan Illich called "sounding pages." If we read aloud what we have written, our breath carries our words into the air. We feel and almost taste the sounds as we shape them with our tongues, teeth, and lips. Writing may be the most completely sensuous of all the arts. How far it can be removed from bodily presence and from the bodily presence of people together, speakers and hearers in a settled community, and still function as language is a lively question.

Insofar as it involves language, literacy is communal. Insofar as it depends upon reading, Ivan Illich was right in seeing that it depends also upon "private space," which is to say solitude, and "periods of silence." I have been depending on and quoting from Illich's book, *In the Vineyard of the Text,* in which he made a beautiful analogy: for a reader to "face a book," preparing to read, is like sitting in a Gothic church in the dark, looking at a window that seems only a part of a wall. And then the dawn comes. The light passes through the window, brightening the colors and the forms of a story. ■

1 More information about the Carnegie Center for Literacy and Learning and the Kentucky Writers Hall of Fame can be found at www.carnegiecenterlex.org.

THE STRIP MINE GIRL

as told by R Hedge

You won't find me up there again, not after that time
when I was a kid when I went there to get away
from the world's watchful eye. There's always been
talk of superstition, due in part to those old grave
stones left unhinged by corporations.
The story was there's this wounded girl running
from a pack of wild-headed men.
And if you saw her, bad things were bound to happen.
I saw her, late at night, passing over that decimated
earth. There in the beams of my headlights,
she was high-tailing it. Now, it could've been
that all I saw was a raccoon or a possum scavenging
the land for food. But what I saw looked to be the
shape of a girl, and I felt myself shiver.
Nothing bad happened. But still, if I consider that
form's true nature, my whole sense of the world
shakes loose. Then, I don't know what to think.
Her dark hair and pale limbs dangling. There,
where the earth had been peeled back, I saw her sunken face.

MATTHEW HAUGHTON

STILL LIFE
IN TOWNSEND

MELANIE K. HUTSELL

1.

Stevie Gibson never did like the picture, but she never did take it down. A dead pheasant still fully feathered, a bowl of oranges, a green glass goblet of wine, and an hourglass were arranged upon a pale tablecloth of folds and wrinkles, all against a shadowed background. She saw that picture every day that she sat behind the computer at her father's heavy oak desk and typed figures for Gibson's Motor Lodge into the Excel spreadsheets. The dark painting had not given her nightmares as a girl but still had pressed against her restless soul whenever she wandered into her father's office. Now the picture was like the wall or the telephone, no different from the hook where she hung her coat or sweater half the year. It came with the job. Luman Gibson still owned every nail in the building, though he lived twenty miles away in an old folks' home in Maryville and did not remember her face or her name. She would not mind to change things around, maybe, but that cost money and took time she did not have. And the things were not hers to change.

2.

The motorcycle couple wore red bandanas on their heads and American flags on their T-shirts and jackets. Stevie manned the front desk of the family business in Townsend, Tennessee. She shared the no-excuses way the motorcycle couple wore their clothes. At thirty-nine, she appeared not much different from the girl who had first been kissed in Tuckaleechee Caverns, who carried big, wide, deep-living dreams when she left Townsend at eighteen. She still wore unforgiving jeans and daredevil necklines. But crow's feet now printed themselves on her face, and grey strands threaded through her spiked blonde hair.

Stevie took the key from the hand of the bearded, booted fellow, as she had from thousands of other hands, and told the man and the woman to enjoy their trip. Several weeks ago, the Wears Valley forest fires all over the national news might have seemed to menace the couple's bike trip down from Michigan. But those fires had burned on the Sevier County side, closer to Pigeon Forge and fought by firefighters from three counties.

The forest fires were out now. Outside and where she could not see, trees had turned to ashes, and the mountain slopes stood charred.

Behind the front desk, Stevie watched the motorcycle man and woman push the glass door and walk on through. They were able to do that, to step into the sunshine and push on up the road.

3.

Stevie Gibson had never not known this house on the hillside. She had known it before its dishwasher, before the bathroom downstairs. Luman placed window units in four rooms when Stevie was in high school. Before that, they turned lights off, opened windows, and sat outside on the porch. Her father had made the clothesline for her mother, sawing wood and pouring concrete so clothes could dry crisp and sweet, keeping the house cooler. A row of white pines at the edge of the yard was not there once. As a girl, Stevie dug holes for the roots though she did not dream to linger in Townsend with them.

In the last of the summer heat, tourists meandered biking paths on either side of the highway below the house. Around them towered mighty folds of the Smoky Mountains, draped in foliage lush and miraculous with sunshine. Nearly all who came to Townsend believed that they looked upon an ancient wilderness. But over a hundred years before, Stevie knew now, the mountains had been logged until they stood naked as the moon. All those great trees now rooted on the slopes and stretching for the sky—the trees that, growing up, she had thought as permanent as the earth—were nothing but new growth, a moment in the life of a mountain.

4.

Plenty of pictures in the Gibson photo album featured Stevie and her best friend, Misty. In Kodak snapshots, the two girls theatrically posed on lawn chairs by the motel pool in the summer. The pony-tailed girls rode red bikes down Old Walland Highway towards the cabins of Sunshine. The grinning girls waved sparklers against the dark.

But the pictures her father had taken and her mother catalogued did not capture every moment of Stevie's girlhood in Townsend. They did not show all the rock climbing, horse-riding, river-tubing days. They did not reveal the high school nights she rolled yards with friends, drank the boys in her class under the table. She had never wanted to give up her freewheeling life for anyone.

Misty Headrick married in the summer after high school. Stevie had packed up her clothes into her father's old '67 Mustang and moved herself on.

Now Stevie closed that album and shelved it high on the wall in Luman Gibson's house.

5.

The head housekeeper of Gibson's Motor Lodge for thirty-seven years, Millicent Badgett texted her grandson on a sleek, shiny smartphone, her grey head bowed. Seated near the older woman in the break room, Stevie wolfed down a cold country ham biscuit and listened to the small television as it broadcast fiery rioting in Europe. Conflagrations were everywhere around her, more news than would ever fit on that television screen. Two more restaurants had closed in as many months. Two more families would be eating beans and the contents of neighbors' extra cans. Millicent had told Stevie also about Piedad Gonzalez, the new hire in housekeeping. It was said the woman had left behind, in a nameless town in Texas, her only child, a little bright-eyed girl. Somehow—Stevie did not know how—that woman went to bed at night, woke up in the morning, cleaned toilets and emptied trash when her daughter was no more than a voice beamed from tower to tower, when the woman could not even touch her own child's hair.

Stevie had not told Millicent that it got harder all the time to make the figures in the spreadsheets add up the way she needed. She had a staff of eleven, an ailing father, and a six-year old daughter herself. The motor lodge kept them all alive. It would be a dark end for the place to become a lifeless hull, crumbled and rotted like so many other abandoned motels with empty parking lots in Townsend, overgrown slowly by young trees.

6.

The young, long-haired girl stood in high, golden grass in the autumn afternoon and watched cars roll down the road. Mules ate grass in the tilted lot just the other side of the barbed wire fence. Down by the river and across the highway stood the Subway.

This was not the ocean. This was another world, moon-far, lonesome and strange, majestic and new. To a transplant child, it was slowly becoming home.

7.

Sloane Lucinda Gibson's crayon art covered every surface of Luman's old refrigerator. Brightly smiling stick people held hands beneath palm trees and stood in exclamation beside rolling waves. Stevie had moved to Myrtle Beach after years of living in towns all over the south as a waitress, as a motel clerk, as whatever suited and paid her. But numberless Coronas and one hot night on the sand had changed Stevie into something altogether new, a mother at thirty-three. She still did not know just how that suited her.

An oven mitt, a small bowl of orange peel, and an empty pizza box lay on the kitchen counter. Finishing a slice or two of orange, Stevie worked on the checkbook at the dinner table, as Sloane Lucinda slept upstairs in Stevie's old bed. Misty, her old friend, kept and fed her child the three nights a week that Stevie drove the miles to see her father. Only on the weekends did Stevie sometimes get to make crusty grilled cheese sandwiches cut in triangles, homestyle green beans that had grown in a neighbor's garden, and thick-cut potatoes fried up just the way her father had always fixed them. She was tired of all she missed.

Fixed to the refrigerator with a Rock City magnet, there among the little-girl handprints like starfish and seaweed, was a single photograph of Sloane Lucinda, four years old and on her tricycle, as she pedaled down the sidewalk in front of the motor lodge. The picture had been taken not long after the move. The Greek restaurant where Stevie hostessed in Myrtle Beach had closed two weeks before the news of Luman Gibson's stroke. Her father had been sitting at his desk, facing the still life on his office wall, balancing the ledger.

8.

Stevie turned tired eyes from the slender, silver maple outside her office window and skimmed them past the painting. In the doorway stood Millicent Badgett, carrying bags of lunch, and Sloane Lucinda in overalls, with blonde hair in dog-ears. Grass stains were on Sloane's denim knees, and her face was full of sun. Stevie herself had waited at that threshold with Millicent through the years, looking to find her father across the room's distance.

The little, wiggling girl spread her arms. Stevie said hello. She turned herself near, leaned forward in the contoured chair with wheels that her daughter loved to move.

9.

The sun slipped down the sky behind the motor lodge, behind Luman Gibson's house next door. The tops of the mountains across the river turned to gold. Stevie sat in the old wooden rocker and watched it happen. She lilted the rocker that carried herself and Sloane Lucinda forward and back, forward and back. Such moments were so fleeting anymore. Her hand rested on the curve of her child's head, which smelled of soap bubbles, and the little girl sprawled small arms around her. A September wind eddied the sound of live music down from Headrick's up the road like a whirl of red and gold leaves. She absorbed the sounds of evening, so familiar, the briskness, the seasonal change. Slowly Stevie and her daughter turned to silhouettes as the buildings of Townsend darkened into the great folds of mountains. Down the highway a steady push of single cars slid along with a rush and pulse that could be the breaking of waves somewhere. Headlights swept through the gathering dark, the flash and sparkle marking the passage of so many lives, evanescent, moving all the time. ■

AN *APPALACHIAN HERITAGE* INTERVIEW

DAVID JOY

David Joy is only thirty-one, but come March, this North Carolina writer will see his first novel, *Where All the Light Tends to Go,* published by Putnam. The book, a gritty tale of "a young man seeking redemption," is highly anticipated and has garnered advance praise from the likes of bestselling novelists Ron Rash, Daniel Woodrell, and Silas House. Rash, one of Joy's mentors from his days as an undergraduate in the literature program at Western Carolina University, has hailed the book as "a fine addition to the country noir vein of Southern literature."

In this interview with *Appalachian Heritage* editor Jason Howard, Joy discusses preparing for the novel's release, confounding stereotypes about Appalachian literature, and why writing is like digging clay.

■ ■ ■

JASON HOWARD: Your debut novel, *Where All the Light Tends To Go,* will be out very soon. How have you been preparing for its release and book tour?

DAVID JOY: Until this past year, I'd never been out of the South, never really been out of North Carolina, and certainly never been on an airplane. Some folks like traveling, but as soon as I get on flat land I start getting anxious. I found my place on this earth and I'd be just fine sitting here until I die. All of this to say, I'm doing everything I can do not to think about it. The book coming out is exciting and there are a whole lot of great things happening and I'm incredibly thankful. I couldn't have wound up in better hands. I have a wonderful agent who stuck by me and found the right editor. The team at Putnam is the best in the business, but, more than that, they're all genuinely kind people. I trust them and I've put myself in their hands. But having a book come out on that type of stage leaves you very exposed. The truth of it is that I'm absolutely scared to death.

JH: The book is set in North Carolina, and one of the characters runs a meth ring while another turns to violence. As you know, Appalachia is often stereotyped

as a violent, drug-ravaged, poverty-stricken region. Did you worry about falling prey to this image of the region in creating these characters and dealing with these issues? How did you walk this tightrope?

DJ: This is a big question...There is a drug epidemic in Appalachia, just as there is educational issues and vocational limitations and a host of other systemic problems that have existed for a long time. To the rest of America, this is the only thing they see reported about this region. They see it on the news and they watch reality television shows like *Moonshiners* or *Appalachian Outlaws* or a documentary like *The Wild and Wonderful Whites of West Virginia* and that becomes Appalachia. That's where the stereotype is rooted. The reality is that while these problems exist, they don't define us, and I think that's why we get so defensive. At the same time, I think dismissing these things is just as problematic as using that stereotype to encapsulate an entire region and a people. At the very least we need to take these opportunities to initiate conversation.

I think it's dangerous to ever talk in universalities. I can walk out my front door in the heart of Jackson County and take you to visit a man who still digs ramps and branch lettuce, a man who predicts the weather based on how the fat rises and sinks in a jar of bear meat. I can take you just over the mountain from there to a place where addicts are trading stolen goods for methamphetamine and oxycontin, or show you a house where a man was tortured to death. Then there's a woman in town who left the mountains and got a law degree, a daughter of farmers who got an education and came back to open a law firm. There are kids at the southern end of the county whose parents are millionaires from Florida, kids born and bred in the mountains in gated communities on Tom

Fazio designed golf courses. These are all different truths of a single place. These are all Appalachian stories. The problem doesn't lie in the truth of it, but in an attempt to universalize that truth. It's extremely dangerous to try and define a region and a people, especially one that stretches as vast geographically as this one. Western North Carolina, where I live, is a lot different from East Tennessee or Kentucky.

As for why I write the types of stories I write, it boils down to the type of literature I'm drawn to. I've always preferred the stories in a collection like Ron Rash's *Burning Bright* to those in *Chemistry and Other Stories*. I like Larry Brown's *Father and Son* more than I like *The Rabbit Factory*. I idolize writers like William Gay and Daniel Woodrell and Donald Ray Pollock and Padgett Powell and these are the types of stories they tell. As an artist, you can't let the fear of propagating a stereotype stop you. We can use the art to spur a conversation about social issues, but, at the end of the day, writers need to practice their craft fearlessly. That's the only way it will be any good.

JH: You have a second novel, *Waiting on the End of the World*, already in the can and tentatively scheduled for publication in 2016. What's it about?

DJ: I've become really interested in ideas of trauma and how the things we witness come to govern our lives. I'm really fascinated by what leads people to do the things they do. A lot of times when we see something on the news, especially something violent or some type of atrocity, we're very quick to pass judgment without ever considering what triggered people to make the decisions they made. In this new novel, I'm playing around with that idea. I've tried to create backstories that become the decision makers for why these characters are doing the things they're doing. So I've got three characters who are haunted, each of them carrying a tremendous weight, and I threw them into a really destructive scenario to see what would happen. With that trigger, the idea was that there were two best friends, Aiden McCall and Thad Broom, who go to buy drugs and wind up witnessing the accidental suicide of their dealer. All of a sudden, a riot of meth and money lands in their laps. That was the set up. Then it was just a matter of watching what happened.

JH: You're in your early thirties and your first two novels are being released by a major publisher. How has this changed your life?

DJ: As far as lifestyle, nothing's changed. I spend far too much time at the bar and stay inside my head entirely too long. I drink too much and sleep too little. So none of that's changed and I don't think it ever will. But as far as process, I'm just having to stay focused and work harder. When you don't have a publishing contract, writing a novel is a lot easier. You've got all the time in the world and you're not worried about what other folks might think. You hope people will read your work, but deep down you know they probably won't, and so you're writing it mostly for yourself. There's a freedom in that. There's something really nice about that kind of freedom. Publishers, on the other hand, are focused on what's next. They have to be. They're looking at things from a business perspective and when a book comes out there's going to be a wave that comes in at first, but that wave is going to recede. They need another wave coming in. There's a sort of tidal ebb and flow for relevancy. That's how you build an audience and that's how they make money. The dream for them is to have a writer who is producing a book a year, and that's really hard for someone who is trying to write literary fiction, someone who'd be happy if they ever write one good book. I'm just having to focus a lot more on the work. If you want to make a real honest-to-god run at things, you have to put in the hours.

JH: When did you know that you wanted to be a writer?

DJ: My parents always kept this old typewriter under one of the end tables in the living room when I was a kid, and my earliest memories writing are on that machine. I couldn't have been more than five, but my mom said that I was writing before I could spell. I'd sit at that typewriter and dictate stories to her and have her tell me which keys to press to spell the words. I can still remember the sound of it and the way it smelled. So I always wanted to write. The difference between those who want to write and those who do write boils down, as with most things, to those who are willing to suffer through not being very good and continue to put in the work. Persistence. There are tons and tons of talented writers, much more talented than I'll ever be, but there are few people stubborn enough to put in the work. Most writers I really admire tend to agree that it takes about ten years of work, or somewhere around a thousand pages, to get anywhere close to decent. The first thousand I wrote were kept in shoeboxes. One day I called my mom and had her douse those boxes with gasoline and torch them in the burn barrel. All of it was bad writing that I needed to get out of my system, but once it was out I never needed to see it again. I'm probably well past two thousand pages now and still not anywhere close to what I'd consider good. I've never been a quick study.

JH: What was the first piece of Appalachian literature you read? How did it affect you?

DJ: I grew up in a storytelling tradition with a grandmother bringing Jack Tales out of Wilkes County. I can't speak about the prevalence of those stories elsewhere in Appalachia, but they're very important to the North Carolina mountains and so I think even as a kid I was surrounded by that type of story. As far as the first piece of Appalachian literature I remember reading, it was probably Silas House's *A Parchment of Leaves*. I think I was still in high school when I read that. I just remember being spellbound by the poetics of his language. There's a section of that novel where Vine is going to bury Aaron's body after she killed him, and that scene just haunted the hell out of me. I still have that section marked in the book: "The trees was bare limbed, and when I looked up, the sky was big and black, speckled with just a few stars, dim but pulsing. I looked at them, taking big gulps of air and knowing that there most certainly was a God, and He was looking at me. I wondered what He thought about it. I wondered what else He expected me to do. And then I doubted God, for I could not understand how He could have let this happen to me. I felt like screaming out. He was watching, though. I was sure of this much." That voice and that type of weight, I knew that's what I wanted to try to do with my life.

JH: I know that you're a big music lover. How does music inform your own writing and creative life?

DJ: I think most writers are obsessed with music. Some of my favorite things William Gay ever wrote were the essays about music in places like *Paste* or *Oxford American*. Silas writes a lot about it. Folks like Ron Rash and George Singleton are really sharp. If you want to get a writer talking, talk about that. There are plenty of days when I might not read, but there's not a day that goes by that I'm not listening to music. All of my best memories, from my dad playing Willie Nelson on the record player to my grandmother singing old hymns, are tied to songs. With my writing, I really like to attach songs to characters. In that first novel, the song that defined that main character was Townes Van Zandt's "Rex's Blues." With this novel I just finished, the song was Blaze Foley's "If I Could Only Fly." I really like doing that. I think it gives you an avenue into the character's soul, and, when you've been away from the story for a while, it gives you a place to reenter.

JH: You also write creative nonfiction, and your memoir *Growing Gills: A Fly Fisherman's Journey* was published in 2011 by a small independent press. Do you approach fiction and creative nonfiction differently? What's it like to move between two genres?

DJ: Early on, and I mean as far as once I was taking my writing seriously, all I wrote was creative nonfiction. What was really strange, though, is that even then, I knew I was moving toward fiction. I knew I wanted to write novels. So I wrote two books of nonfiction, only one of which found a publisher, and then that shift that I'd been anticipating happened. I'll still write an essay now and then, but, for the most part, I find myself writing less and less nonfiction. I'm still really interested in it and I still read a good bit of it, but I don't think I'm very good at what I admire most in good nonfiction, especially good memoir. I just read an incredible memoir by an Appalachian writer named Leigh Ann Henion called *Phenomenal* that's coming out of Penguin. One of the things I love most about that memoir is her ability to self assess and just the brutal honesty of it. I think the people who are masters of that form, someone like Rick Bragg, have something I lack. That type of nonfiction takes bravery. I think sometimes I'm scared to turn over the rock because I fear what I'll find squirming around in there.

JH: You count among your writing mentors Pamela Duncan, Deidre Elliott, and Ron Rash. That's a fine list of names. How important have they been to your development as a writer? What have you learned from each of them?

DJ: All three of them are family and I'll never be able to repay them.

Ron was the first person to ever read any of my writing. He wasn't a teacher of mine at the time and the way it happened is that someone just kind of dropped me in his lap. It was a story called "The Legend of Willie Simmons and the Uncatchable Fish," and it was absolutely terrible. But that story got us talking about fishing and we became quick friends. I've learned a lot from him about writing, but what I've learned most from him is about work ethic and just how to be a good man. He was raising two kids with a wife and working some crazy class load at a community college when he wrote those stories in *The Night the New Jesus Fell to Earth*. He was getting up before the sun and putting in hours. He's just a workhorse and always has been. He works harder than anyone I've ever known. But he's also one of the kindest and humblest men I've had the privilege to know. The way he carries himself and the way he cares about people, that's what I love about him. That's what will hang with me for the rest of my life.

With Deidre Elliott, she's one of the most talented creative nonfiction writers I've ever read, but she's by far the best teacher I ever had. She'd take someone with little talent and get something publishable out of them. She pushed people to their absolute best. That's who taught me craft. That's who showed me how to take a draft and keep reworking the language and reworking the language until you make music. I'll owe every single thing I ever write to Deidre.

As for Pam, she and I became friends when I'd finished that first book of nonfiction, *Growing Gills*. I actually wrote that in graduate school and Pam served on my thesis committee. I learn things from her every time I see her. She's who gave me the idea of using songs as entry into characters. She's who told me that my new novel was about trauma. She'll never lead on like it, but she's one of wisest souls I know. She knows as much about writing as anybody. She's scary talented.

JH: I've read that you've compared the writing process to digging clay. What do you mean by that?

DJ: When I was growing up, my mother was a potter, and one of the things I admired most about her was that she made mistakes beautiful. Her process was fluid. If something didn't work out, she just rolled with it and molded it into something new. I never was like that. I just wasn't that patient. So when I was little I would spend all day drawing and if I made a mistake I'd tear it up and start again. I'd do this over and over until I eventually got it perfect. The problem is that doesn't work with something like a novel. Novels are made in the revisions. If you spend your time focusing on sentence level issues in the early drafts, you'll never get anything done. You can't make a pot until you have the clay. There's a process to it. You don't just grab a handful of mud out of the bank and try to make art. You dig the clay, then you process that clay to remove the extraneous material, then you wedge the clay, and then eventually, eventually you can make a pot. Writing a novel is just like that. Those early drafts are digging clay, and digging clay is hard work. Revising is when you get to sit down at the wheel and turn a pot, though if we're going with this metaphor mine is more like slab work or maybe pinch pots. I'm not very graceful and my pots always wind up lopsided. ■

REMOVAL ACT: JOHN YOUNG SQUIRREL

1838

Soldiers pound the door with bayonets, pound
while John Young Squirrel tends his baby son,
pound while his small daughter eats corn-cake
smeared with bear grease, while the boy gums
John's little finger. His wife gone to Turkey-town

to midwife for her sister, soldiers pound and a fear
speaks to him, tatter of smoke, ragged shadow
that whispers, snarls, *your wife lost, never find her.*
Sometimes border-whites grab a woman, pry open
her mouth, force liquor in, their version of mercy,

knock her senseless, sometimes the woman is given
nothing that stuns, sometimes soldiers rape first,
rape any they catch, rape again. Set you on fire,
soldiers shout, and John grabs walnuts, corn-cake,
a pail of milk, gives his daughter a few potatoes,

ties his son to his chest with his wife's binding-cloth.
His son squirms as he walks. His daughter
trots along, her eyes trained on some far thing
John can't see. He watches the soldiers' bayonets.
The fear says, *all of you stabbed.* John tells the fear,

not these two. His son kicks his ribs, he almost falls,
the pail sloshes, does not spill. At the next farm,
two soldiers guard John and his children

in a meadow while many more soldiers scream,
charge the cabin. John unties the binding-cloth,
wets the corner with milk, feeds his son,
then he and his daughter drink from the pail.
The fear says, *they will starve.* John says,
if they give us no food, these two will eat the air,
grow stronger each day. While soldiers

round up the people, his son pops a bit of twig
into his mouth, John doesn't know what to do,
should he swing the boy by the feet, slap his back,
squeeze his chest—but then his son coughs hard,
spits out the twig. Soldiers set fire to the cabin,

corn-crib, and winter-house, flames hiss,
bayonets glint. His daughter hands him
a red berry she picked from the weeds
at his feet—not goatsbeard, as he thought,
but a plant hiding fruit under its dull leaves.

WILLIAM KELLEY WOOLFITT

SHALL CLEAVE UNTO

A man, a woman, a husband,
a wife, both had been slaves of
Cherokee planters, both of mixed
descent, him more African, the dark
of mourning bombazine, her more
Cherokee, the gold of tafia rum,
both learned to read at the mission school, his master gave
 him some hogs,
hers let her take in dressmaking,
both saved to buy themselves
free, her first time off the plantation
hog-catching with him, him trying
the fine coat she tailored for his master
you're as big as he she said

your hand, fine stitches, sharp eye
he said, him manumitted first, her next
when he borrowed ahead to finish
the note, both renting a few rough
acres from Johnson, both hoeing,
hauling away stones, more stones,
still more stones, both grabbed
by soldiers, prodded down the road
into the clamor and dust of herded
people dogs cows horses keening bawling
groaning, so many horses, eyes
fearful ears flat frothing with sweat,
buckskins crackers piebalds
men women boys girls spat on

goaded kicked jabbed with bayonets
both crest a hill, see the wall of logs
where all the people are amassed
her at the stockade door shoved in
him sorted out pushed with horses
into livestock pens, him struggling
to climb out, thrashing at soldiers,
him stripped whipped lifting his arms
while buyers inspect his limbs and
extremities, count his teeth, at a gap
in the logs, her casting her eyes
for him, thinking it's him, her mouth
at a gap, him leaning as he tips his head,
hears her perhaps call his name

WILLIAM KELLEY WOOLFITT

LUCK OF THE DRAW

ELAINE FOWLER PALENCIA

When the doorbell rang that early January afternoon in 1967, Florene Mullins had just turned on the two table lamps in the living room. The winter day was shading into twilight and shadows pooled in the corners, making her feel blue. She was considering fixing pork chops and fried potatoes for supper. A good, substantial meal, she thought. That would cheer them both up. Bill had taken sardines and crackers with him for lunch.

She opened the front door to find Roy McCoy Jr. standing on the porch. He had a folded newspaper tucked under his arm.

"Hello. Come in," she said, confused. She had known Roy for years, but he had never been in their house, nor they in his. What did he want? Roy was a rich man. He was dressed for the bank, in suit and tie.

"How do, neighbor. Wonder if I could take a minute of your time," said Roy, stepping inside and looking around with interest.

The house smelled of bacon, wood ash, and laundry detergent. It was the smell of his early life in the neighborhood. As a boy, he had played in and out of all these houses. His grandfather, Roy Morgan McCoy, who made his money in timber, had built every home between Crescent Boulevard, along which the college ranged, and Main Street to the south. The more substantial homes, the ones he built for his own family members, were on the edges of the area, with bigger lawns and better views. Roy Junior lived in one of those.

"Bill's not here. He's working up in Grayson today," Florene said. This was most unusual, having a man of Roy's status call at the house. People said the Governor was going to nominate him for some state commission. "Won't you sit down?"

McCoy sat on the oxblood Naugahyde sofa and put the newspaper on the coffee table in front of him. "I don't need to talk to Bill."

"Would you like some coffee?"

"That'd be nice."

Florene hurried to the kitchen. Why had she offered coffee, when she was out of drip? It would have to be instant, a humiliation. In despair she filled the kettle at the sink, turned on the stove, and set the kettle on the flame.

They were keeping up with the mortgage payments, she thought to herself. Maybe it was about the hedge. Blue Valley was a small town, squashed between the eastern Kentucky hills, so that rich and not-so-rich lived together with little separation. The imposing house and grounds of Roy's father Ben, who was president of the bank where Roy was vice-president, shared a property line with the Mullins's side yard. The overgrown hedge along the line, which technically was in the Mullins's yard, threw suckers into the elder McCoy's grass. Could you be sued for that?

In the living room, Roy rolled his shoulders to loosen them, thinking of how he used to warm up when he pitched for the Tolliver High and Blue Valley College baseball teams.

The house smelled of bacon, wood ash, and laundry detergent. It was the smell of his early life in the neighborhood.

He and Florene had been in an English class together in college. She was a quiet, self-possessed girl from Breathitt County. Smooth brown hair with a mild natural wave, serious hazel eyes, neat and efficient in her movements. Not silly or flashy like the girls he usually picked, and therefore both interesting and a little frightening. When the professor called on her, she would generally give an intelligent answer based on her own opinion, not on the textbook. This was a revelation to Roy. In literature, unlike in accounting, you were allowed to make up your own mind about class material. For half a semester he gathered courage to ask her out; and then, just when he had the words ready, he learned she was engaged. Bill Mullins was older, a lanky, flirtatious salesman at Marty's Appliances with a line as cheap as Marty's washing machines. Roy had heard him bragging about his conquests at the pool hall, though never about Florene.

Roy surveyed the loose-weave beige curtains hanging limply at the windows on either side of the sooty fieldstone fireplace, the wood floor in need of refinishing, the brown ceramic table lamps from the Green Stamps catalog—he knew because his tight-fisted cousin Mary had a pair just like them. A pencil line crack zigzagged up the wall from the right corner of the fireplace to the ceiling. Florene had a decent job teaching junior high, but he'd heard that Bill had a gambling problem.

Florene returned with a blue aluminum tray bearing two cups of coffee, a sugar bowl, a creamer, and a plate of Fig Newtons. She moved aside the newspaper, set down the tray, and took a seat in the brown corduroy armchair opposite Roy.

"Cream?" she asked hopefully. It would mask the taste.

He shook his head and said pleasantly, "I saw Vickie in the bank the other day with your grandbaby. Cute as a button. How old is she?" He bit into a Newton. His wife Jackie had banned cookies from their house until she lost seven pounds.

Florene said, "Tresia's nearly two." She picked up her cup and set it back down.

"Vickie and Brad doing all right?"

"Oh, yes. He's with Falk Motors." She remembered that her daughter and son-in-law had gotten their house loan at McCoy's bank, too. Had something gone wrong there?

"And Terry? He's doing all right in college?"

"Well, he finished his first semester, more or less. But he didn't take to it."

McCoy sat forward. "How do you mean?"

"Oh, I don't know. College algebra gave him fits. And at that age you want to get out and see the world. Cut the apron strings. He's down in Bogalusa, Louisiana."

"Doing what?" McCoy demanded, as if he had a relative's right to know.

"Working on the pipeline. He kind of likes it down there, says it's different. They eat crawdads." She smiled, but quit when she saw how serious McCoy looked.

"Terry was the best third baseman Tolliver ever had. He ought to go out for the college team. They need somebody in the hot corner this year." Dumb kid, he thought. Quitting school at a time like this.

"He hasn't mentioned trying out," said Florene.

Terry Mullins had the same grace and style on the diamond that he, Roy, had in his day. If there was one thing that Roy loved better than making money, it was boys for whom sports came easily. His two sons, Jamie and Davie, eleven and nine, were more like their mother, always too hot or too cold to do much outside. They played sports like, well, children. No real sense of competition or of the romance of the game. When they were small, he'd played pitch and catch with them in the backyard and had taken them to the Louisville Slugger factory and to see the Reds play in Cincinnati. To little avail, as far as he could see. They thought it was all just "fun."

Florene relaxed. Maybe Roy wanted a donation for some charity. She could spare a little something.

He gave the newspaper between them a quarter turn so that it was squarely facing her. "Listen here. He needs to get back in school. He's going to get back in school, do you understand? It doesn't matter about playing ball. He needs to come back and register for the second semester. Now." He looked at her intently, then drew her eyes with his to the coffee table.

The World section of the *Blue Valley News* was on top. Florene saw a headline: "Vietnam: Land of War, Land of Contrasts."

She felt a physical shift in her skull, as if the blood in her brain had solidified. Oh, my God, she thought. Roy was not only the vice-president of the bank and president of the hospital steering committee. He was also head of the draft board.

She swallowed hard. "I'll see he does it. I appreciate—."

"Don't mention it. I mean, really. Don't mention it," said Roy, and saw that she understood both the seriousness of the issue and the need to remain silent about his visit.

At church, Roy sang baritone in the choir next to Devin Fields, the college registrar. A couple of weeks later, Fields was able to assure him that Terry Mullins was in school again. Roy felt good. He had made a difference and no one need know. That showed true spiritual humility, which he knew he needed to work on. He did allow himself the private pleasure of sharing a secret with Florene Mullins, and of keeping it from Jackie. He couldn't share secrets with his wife. Telling her was like telling CBS. In an hour the whole town would know.

Months passed, and the bank auditors came and he forgot all about Terry Mullins.

He couldn't share secrets with his wife. Telling her was like telling CBS. In an hour the whole town would know.

About a year later, coming out of Baird Drug, he ran into Bruiser Jones. Since his retirement from Buildings and Grounds at the college, Bruiser fished, worked in his garden, and roamed around town finding out things.

Bruiser tilted back his old grey fedora and fixed Roy with his good eye. "Well, reckon we lost another one. That makes three from here. With this Tet Offensive thing, I severely doubt it'll be the last."

"Say what?" said Roy.

With his fat tongue Bruiser rolled his perpetually unlit cigar from the right corner of his mouth to the left. "The Dishman boy. Quang Tri Province. Small arms fire."

Roy felt his hair stiffen. He'd substituted the name Jody Dishman for that of Terry Mullins without any trouble from the rest of the board. In fact, they hadn't quite realized what he was up to. Someone did mention that Jody was from out in the county and worked at the lumberyard. Neither college bound nor a tradesman.

"How do you know this?" Roy asked.

"It'll be hard on his daddy," mused Bruiser. "He's nearly blind from that accident, lives alone since the wife died. Jody was awful good to go over there and help him out." Suddenly his wandering eye swung around and nailed Roy. "Luck of the draw, I guess. Be seeing you." He drifted off towards the pool hall.

That evening, Roy poured himself two inches of bourbon and took the glass into the patio room on the back of the house. His doctor allowed him one inch per day; he allowed himself the other. Jackie had taken the boys to a school play. He sat down in a wicker armchair next to one of the big windows.

Along the rail fence that bordered the back yard, jonquils glowed like a string of footlights. The lawn was a vivid green and shrubs were furring out. Spring was early: the world was coming back to life.

He knocked back the bourbon and felt sweat spring out along his hairline. He couldn't get down on himself or it would affect the way he made decisions at the bank. Of course he had realized that to replace Terry was to put some other young man in harm's way. He'd known that from the beginning or he wouldn't have been so careful about it. But he hadn't imagined a real person shot with real bullets. And anyway, how could he have foreseen the Tet Offensive? You couldn't predict what would happen in a war.

What was a man supposed to do? Terry had been their paperboy. He was from the neighborhood. When you could, you took care of your own. It happened in every war. He'd had a desk job during Korea; Senator Hall had taken care of that. Otherwise, what was the point of having money and influence?

Gradually the light died. Street sounds diminished, leaving the muttering of the creek beyond the fence. He sat in the dark. After a while, he heard the front door open. The boys clattered upstairs to their rooms, shouting and laughing. He felt Jackie's hand on his shoulder.

"Davie did a good job. He remembered all his lines," she said, and set a hip on the arm of his chair.

"Good," he said.

"He was Henry Clay. It was a historical pageant."

"Great," said Roy.

"Not that you give a care."

"What's that supposed to mean?"

She stood and turned on the overhead light, which she knew he hated. Squinting against the glare, Roy looked up at her. The pale lipstick paired with heavy mascara, some new look from England, made her face look like a mask.

"If it was one of your blessed committees you would have found the time," she said, and walked out of the room.

The newspaper printed a picture of Jody Dishman in uniform along with his obituary. He was survived by his father, an aunt and uncle, and a fiancée.

Soon another Moore County boy died. At the college, students marched against the war. Roy changed the way he drove to the bank, so he wouldn't pass the campus. He decided that Jackie was right. He needed to show up for his boys more often. But when he tried to watch a Little League game, watch the tender bodies of the children trying to ape the movements of grown-ups, he would be overcome with a terrible need to cry. Rather than make a fool of himself, he would leave the bleachers and stand in the parking lot until he had his control back. He missed whole innings that way. At home, when his sons were slow to do their few chores, he shouted at them and withheld allowances.

"What is wrong with you?" Jackie would hiss, but he couldn't answer.

Jamie and Davie began to look at him differently, their clear eyes clouding with hurt and mistrust, like dogs who are getting ready to run away. ■

THE POET'S HOUSE WAS A TRIP

The poet's house was a trip
I could not refuse.

I knew you only through words,
anxious to hear your lyrical wisdom
about meter and muse
the heart of a simple line,
but something more humble
surfaced the poetic journey.

The spreading peach tree in your front yard
almost hid you from our view
as our car pulled to a stop
until you reached up
and offered us the bright fuzzy globes.

We ate until our chins stickied
and our hands dripped sweet
laughter sealing a friendship
like summer to a jar,
memories ripe and ready
for the joyous picking
against the cruel snatch of winter,
fuzzy dreams filling
our eager palms
with nuggets of gold.

ALLISON THORPE

BARREN

I found them the summer I was eight.
The nest took up the entire space
inside the grill. It was a deep crater—
twigs and mud woven into the metal grates.
In the center were two blue eggs.
My mother told me they were robins' eggs.

For weeks, I kept them over my night light,
toilet paper tucked around them
wishing warmth from the tiny bulb would seep
through layers of mud and dried grass to those
blue eggs and the robins I knew were inside.

I would have waited all winter
for baby birds to burst from those shells.
Instead, my cousin broke the eggs open
just before Christmas.
Inside, the remains were caked to the sides of the shell,
dark spots of eye and wing
dried to a yellow-brown crust.

The doctor told me my eggs are just as dry,
all the fertile marrow sucked away
with endometriotic precision.
I hold my secret close,
my fingers cupped around my belly.
I press through layers of organ and warm blood,
touch ovaries, retreat.

KATHRYN CODY

THE SACRED STILLNESS OF FATHER DAMIEN

KATHERINE SCOTT CRAWFORD

I came to the writing of bestselling novelist Louise Erdrich for the first time as a twenty-five-year-old graduate student working towards her Masters of Arts in English. I read what most consider to be her masterwork, *Love Medicine,* for a course in Contemporary American Fiction, and I was at once entranced and disturbed, delighted and dumbfounded by Erdrich's masterful interweaving of the mythical and the modern, and of the dark and light sides of human nature—most especially, of course, when it came to her wildly-forked, fictional family tree of Ojibwe from the reservation of Little No Horse. Outside of the works of Shakespeare, I don't think I've ever encountered so many characters with whom I have both fallen in love, and abhorred, at the same time.

Since that time, I've read and felt much the same way about several of Erdrich's other works—including *Tracks, Four Souls,* and *The Painted Drum*—but none have struck me quite so much as *The Last Report on the Miracles at Little No Horse.* I fell head-over-heels in love with the character of Agnes, who as Father Damien Modeste, has fulfilled her sacred duties to her flock for over fifty years disguised as a man. (To avoid confusion, I'll hitherto refer to Agnes/Father Damien as Father Damien or Damien, and as "her," because, no matter how she chooses to live, in my reader's mind I can't separate her from her female self.) When she hurts for, cares about and despairs over the members of her congregation on the reservation, I find myself inevitably doing the same.

But more than this readerly investment in the plight of these particular characters—something I do find absolutely essential to any enjoyment of any story—I am awed by the periods of "silence" or "stillness" in the novel: by these moments of interiority, with Father Damien especially, when she is considering her place in this community of misfits and wild ones. Though, as Gertrude Stein might assert, here "nothing much happens," so much is invariably revealed—about Damien, about her internal conflicts and the way she views religion and Catholicism, life, death—all the important aspects of her world and the world of the people to whom she ministers.

In his essay "Stillness" from *Burning Down the House,* Charles Baxter juxtaposes this idea of creating—or seeking—

stillness in our fiction with the contrary, quintessentially American urge for action, even violence. There are so many fascinating issues which he raises in this essay that could be connected with *The Last Report of the Miracles at Little No Horse* (or for that matter, with any of Erdrich's novels), like this idea of the modern American need for activity, and the fact that we associate silence "... with madness, mooncalfing, woolgathering, laziness, hostility, and stupidity."[1] There are amazing places one could go with this critically, because of the remnants of ancient Ojibwe traditions and culture that pervade the reservation throughout Damien's time there; the Ojibwe, like many American Indian tribes, value such stillness, such contemplation, and are discouraged and often confused by the erratic pace of the white world. But for the purposes of this essay, I'll stick to what these periods of stillness tell us about Father Damien.

Indeed, most of the novel is focused on the interior thoughts of Damien's (and other characters). In these moments of what I'll call "stillness," Damien is doing incredibly mundane things: writing letters, drinking wine, taking confession, sitting outside in a rocking chair, even playing the piano. I equate these things with stillness, even though Damien may physically move during them, because they are so free from the frenetic sort of action that Baxter mentions, that we American readers tend to fall prey to—and have come to depend on—in our modern novels and movies. But consider Damien here, as an old woman in her last year of life, writing to the Pope yet again:

> *The night was mild, and Father Damien rose to let in that spectral air. He hoisted a small-paned window and the sigh of night-singing grasshoppers and crickets entered his small study. A pure sound, welcome,*

promising a light refreshing rain. Clearing everything away, washing the world innocent. If only he, too, could be washed to perfect goodness, forgiven! Father Damien drank deeply of the old, secret pain, and once more took up the pen.[2]

Here, Erdrich manages—through beginning with a seemingly benign description of a small movement inside the rectory (opening a window to let in the night air)—to convey the deeply-welled intellect of this character. Erdrich moves past Damien's frail outer self and allows us to see and to feel just how wildly this river of guilt (the fact that she is, of course, a woman masquerading as a man—and as a priest) rages inside her.

Later, when her former lover, Father Gregory Wekkle, visits her for the first time in many years, Damien is physically still, at first, upon seeing him, but her thoughts leap with meaning:

As they regarded each other across the uncertain band of dim space just outside the confessional, a thrill of self-consciousness washed over Agnes. Father Damien was not beautiful. Agnes wanted to touch back her hair and bite her lips. The mere thought of such gestures made her cheeks flame red. Then she wanted Father Wekkle to leave, immediately, to leave her to the simple contentment she'd nurtured to replace the great drama of human love. Get out of here! Get thee behind me! she wanted to yell at him.[3]

In this passage, during these moments, Damien has not moved. She wants to act—to do something to make herself look more attractive, to shout at him—but she doesn't follow through on either. The skill of Erdrich's writing is that Damien doesn't need to; there's more power in the fact that she does not act at all. This is one of those times in fiction—"a moment of stillness"—when as Baxter asserts, "the atmosphere supplants the action."[4]

Crafting such moments of stillness in fiction is something with which I most certainly struggle as a writer. So it's the slightest bit reassuring to read that Baxter recognizes that:

> *One has to struggle against the narrative necessities of fiction in order to get a moment of stillness into the story in the first place, and in this struggle, the tendency is to lurch toward overstatement, out of a fear of boring the reader.*[5]

At times, I'm so concerned with crafting the action, or plot, of my novel, that I unintentionally leave out those moments of inaction—those periods of stillness wherein, if I tried, I could possibly reveal the depths of my own characters.

A study of a master of interiority like Erdrich offers much help, for she certainly deals in wonder—an aspect of stillness Baxter finds necessary: "So, finally we arrive at wonder; which, for me, is at the bottom level, the ground floor, of stillness."[6] In fact, it is this feeling of wonder, I believe, that separates Erdrich's writing from so much of the fiction of her contemporaries. And in Damien's last moments of life, her stillness—her actual wonder at life's mysteries and at all that she's experienced—are the greatest of transitions: a transition into death.

> *She sank to her knees and with an amused wonder watched as slowly, with an infinite kindness, darkness covered up the other side as well. Sightless, now, she*

> *sank to earth and felt the heat of the leaping fire on her face. I am going, I am going, she thought. Underneath her and before her, a wide plain of utter emptiness opened. Trusting, yearning, she put her arms out into that emptiness.*[7]

It's another of those moments—those quiet power moments—when not much is actively happening. Damien is merely on her knees, holding out her arms. But, incredibly, the earth is moving, the world is changing, and if we as readers are open to it, so, too, will we. ■

1 Charles Baxter. "Stillness." *Burning Down the House: Essays on Fiction.* (Minneapolis: Graywolf Press, 2008), 175-196.
2 Louise Erdrich. *The Last Report on the Miracles at Little No Horse.* (New York: Perennial, 2002), 5-6.
3 Ibid., 300.
4 Baxter, 181.
5 Ibid., 183-184.
6 Ibid., 195.
7 Erdrich, 349-50.

BEFORE GRACELAND

She got slaps for watching the boys—
slick, khakied, and home for leave—
step off the bus, just in from Fort Benning.
Mildred didn't care. She dressed up
like Judy Tyler to watch *Love Me Tender*
on the black and white Motorola
when her father went to work.
She dreamed she was a shelled pecan
under Elvis's tongue. In the morning,
Mildred counted the flecks of pepper on her eggs,
sipped her juice, and considered the distance
between here and Memphis.

LAUREN ALBIN

HYDRANGEA RIDGE

1.

With chainsaw and sling-blade, we felled pines and hickory,
zinged away brier and poke. Together we string our
squarings.
Dig in with auger, rock-bar, and shovel. Dig to embed

our pole foundation. Each morning the suckerings
bend the squaring lines and another toad squats
in a hole, presiding over the shallow puddle.

We have to lie down to scoop him out. He stays close,
ready to reclaim his deep and narrow kingdom.

2.

The mantis prays on the pane. Above the stove,
webs fill with mosquitoes and moths.

A walking stick strolls over porch screens.
Outside, in the thicket of fleabane daisy

and brier, a tomato volunteered its vine,
bore fruit. Spiny branches shelter it

from hungry deer. When the king snake slipped
away from the house, we called for it to come back,

come back for the kitchen mice, for chipmunks,
for the rattlers that we fear nestling in the woodpile.

3.

A chill rises, the leaves blaze as if to warm
the trees' shivering limbs. We turn, orbiting
closer to the woodstove. From felled trees

we haul rounds to their cradle. We circle
the radiating dark iron, reaching out
to take hold of its heat. Outside, no breeze

stirs, still the bare trees sway, flickering
from all that burns within, the days
of grasping after sun, gleaning its fire.

TINA BRAZIEL

TO SHAKE ANOTHER

When heat visibly wavers over our truck hood,
we feel like puddles, our skin as thin as a frog's.

From the broom sage, the rattle of katydids ripples
through us. I remember first feeling sound

in grade school. Striking a tuning fork, I watched
its slight quaver shake another fork into its own

humming. Evenings then, when pines shivered
with the chirr of peepers, I wondered how frogs carry

quivering metal inside their tenderness. Today pressing
my cheek to our house frame, I hammer listening

to how all the driven nails resound. Each nail stokes
another chord, every joining of metal to wood drapes

the house in melody, unfolding from here to beyond
the ridge. In it, I feel the reverberation of hammer, anvil,

and stirrup of when he first called my name
setting all of me, what is tender and mettle, abuzz.

TINA BRAZIEL

FALL

ADAM PADGETT

The cliff stood before them, their necks turned up, looking upon the seventy feet of tan rock with black iron veins splaying about the stone. *It's about confidence,* Lars had told her. *If you have confidence that you won't fall, then you won't fall.* The girl reached over and played with his belt loop and kissed him on the cheek, not realizing he had used this line on girls before. She tied into the rope and climbed the cliff, nervous but excited at the same time.

Trust. That's what he'd earn. Lars had been teaching rock climbing in the Southern Appalachians for nearly two years and climbing recreationally for over ten. *Twenty-two years old and seeking life,* he'd say to girls. He was seeking life, seeking to live and to see what the world would show him next. A crock of shit, but often, girls would go back to the campsite and Lars would have them there in the cold dewy evening. Water beading on the inside of the tent from their breath.

At some point, however, he stopped telling his friends about the girl he was screwing and told them instead about Julie, who climbed with a natural grace and ability Lars had never seen in someone just starting out. He adored the way she moved and the smell of whatever she washed her dark colored hair with. Lars would say it was black, however she'd call it a very dark brown. She often wore a T-shirt with *PeTA* across her breasts in white lettering atop neon-green cotton. Typically Lars disliked hippies and their brand of ridiculous movements. Telling him to invest in potato-powered cars and to run his microwave off positive juju and good will. But he liked Julie's purple nails and the thin ring that circled around one of her nostrils.

He taught her everything she knew about climbing and taught her well. It wasn't long until she started to finish climbs that had once been projects of his—something he thought incredible. He felt not jealousy, but arousal at the idea. She was gorgeous, small, and strong. Not muscular, just strong. A precocious talent for the sport that'd gone untapped. After a day of climbing, they'd go back to the campground and make love much in the same way. Not rough or violent. Just strong.

He got used to her tie-dye shirts with peace symbols. He grew to enjoy their conversations on love and politics. Inexplicable and stupid, she made him want to be more conscious of high fructose corn syrup and red dye number whatever. Lars hadn't meant for it to, but this thing he had with this girl turned into something of a relationship. They climbed with each other. Only each other. They took falls together, big falls. Surging adrenaline into their brains and into their sex.

He got used to her tie-dye shirts with peace symbols. He grew to enjoy their conversations on love and politics.

He remembered her first big fall. He caught her. She fell about fifteen or twenty feet. It was a soft catch, and, as the rope slowed her decent to an eventual stop, he looked into her wide eyes, thrill and fear. Strands of her hair fanned out from the fall and a few of them stayed that way after the fall. Lars lowered her the rest of the way to the ground and she grabbed his face and pushed her mouth into his. That night it was good. Really good. The best it had been, and it hadn't been as good since. It was the fall. The fall was a reward. Their reward. The fall brought them to life.

■ ■ ■

The two of them lay in the tent, under sleeping bags, holding and feeling the calluses on the other's hands. Skin, thick and stiff. Like imprints left from the rock. "Okay, stop feeling my hand," she said, smiling.

"Why?"

"Because it's gross dead skin."

"So, I've got them too," he said, kissing her neck.

"Girls aren't supposed to have rough hands. It's not ladylike."

“I think it’s hot.”

“You just want to get laid,” she, turning away from his kiss but smiling still.

“Right, but it doesn’t make it any less true.”

She picked up his hand and pulled a piece of lose skin from his palm and held it up so they could see the translucent flake in the headlamp. “See. Gross.” She unzipped the tent and tossed it out to the dirt and zipped the door back up.

Julie rubbed the place where she had pulled the callus and stared thoughtfully at the mangled layer of skin in the palm of her hand.

“What if I got really strong from climbing?” she asked him.

“What do you mean?”

“What if I got really jacked, like crazy muscles and butch. Like those girls in the magazines. Would you still be attracted to me?”

“Yes.”

“Even if I was a freak of nature?”

“Even if you were a freak of nature.”

■ ■ ■

Early spring. The sunlight cooked their skin while the shadows were bitter cold. Their pullovers came on and off on a constant basis, and on the last climb of the day, Lars left his on. He had climbed above the tree line, the wind rendering his hearing useless. There were no pockets or jugs on the cliff, just tiny crimps, thin rails of iron on which to grab using only the pads of his fingers. His forearms had filled with blood and lactic acid, and the feeling was of wires pulling his fingers open. He found himself fifteen feet from his last piece of gear into the wall—looking to a thirty-foot fall should he not place the next soon.

He reached up and crimped his fingers over a hold and the sharpness of brown sandstone dug harshly into his skin. As Lars moved his weight underneath the hold, it crumbled as if made of brittle clay and then he was falling.

On the trip down he felt angry. Angry at the throbbing and exhaustion that had pried his fingers away. At the poor choice to pull on such a thin flake of rock. When he fell, the rope caught and tangled with one of his legs, flipping his body upside down, rotating him away from the wall vertically, 180 degrees, until the back of his head cracked against the stone. When his descent finally stopped, he hung on the bright orange rope, one leg tangled and pointed toward the sky. His head and arms hung toward the ground like something in a meat locker—blood dripping thick from his hair. Julie, on the other end of the rope, caught him. Ten feet from the deck, ten feet from the rocky ground.

It took rescue over two hours to evacuate him. The doctor diagnosed him with a severe concussion and a slight skull fracture, and told him he was lucky that it hadn't been any worse considering he wasn't wearing a helmet. Told him he'd be back on his feet in a couple weeks, gave him several stitches in the head, and then told him to refrain from dangerous activity for a few months.

The severity of the fall was by no means Julie's fault. She did exactly what he taught her. To arrest a fall. To keep him from decking, from hitting the ground. But later, he had asked her anyway. Asked her what happened and to explain herself because, for the life of him, he couldn't remember.

"You just fell," she said. "You just fell and I caught you and when I looked up, you flipped."

"I just fell?"

"Yes, you just fell and I caught you." Tears welled atop her lashes and she turned away from him and wept while she stared at her glass of wine—the first time he had seen her cry.

The months would escape them and they would completely abandon the idea of climbing. As those months drifted and fell away, only fragments of the fall would come back to him. His memory and his body became a kind of obscure puzzle that, if assembled properly, would tell of a truth, though the pieces had been lost and he would not be able to recover them.

■ ■ ■

Skin flaked and peeled considerably from Lars's hands. Old calluses purged, returning his hands to soft.

He and Julie didn't sleep together for a while. They slept in the same bed but not together. The accident took it out of them and he hadn't even realized it until those months later. He felt as though he were still falling, constantly bracing himself for the bottom he would never hit. One night he kissed her neck and reached around, under her shirt to her bellybutton, an act that used to make her horny as all hell. She pushed his hand away without a word. He rolled over, feeling the tenderness still on the back of his skull. So he turned on his stomach and it made his back hurt, but the tender part of his skull didn't touch the pillow, one pain exchanged for another.

■ ■ ■

Early autumn. Charlotte sat miles behind them, and the further they drove on I-77 the longer it'd be to turn around and go back. The Appalachians rose from the earth, their musculature blanketed by brown October trees. They agreed that he'd drive first for a while and then at some point she'd take the wheel. Lars looked at the time on the dash and then at the time on his wrist. He placed a hand on her thigh and told her that he loved her. Julie put her hand atop his and hummed a pleasant hum, not breaking her gaze from the window, the mountains. He put his hand back on the wheel and checked the time again.

They turned into a gas station. The sun was slipping and the mountains cast cold shadows. The temperature change pressed against their skin as he exited the vehicle to pump the gas. In the fifties, but he could still see his breath cloud in front of them. She lowered her window.

“Want food?” Lars asked her, leaning against the car door. Gallons ticking away on the pump.

“No.”

“There’s a Subway here.”

“No. I’d rather go to the Wal-Mart once we get into town. Cheaper.”

He placed a hand on her thigh and told her that he loved her. Julie put her hand atop his and hummed a pleasant hum, not breaking her gaze from the window, the mountains.

“Okay.” He said and turned around with arms crossed. “You know, it’s two hours till that Wal-Mart, right?”

“If you want food, just go. I’ll pump the gas.”

“I’ll wait. We’ll go to Wal-Mart.”

■ ■ ■

After they drove through the second tunnel, Julie stared at the trees as they blew by and the scenery opened to more mountains, more rock. "How do you feel?" she asked after nearly an hour of quiet.

"What do you mean?"

"You. The fall. How do you feel? Feel like you'll do okay?"

"Yeah, fine. Why?"

"Just wondering. Don't really talk much about it."

"You want to talk about it," he replied, his tone not suggestive of a question, though he meant for it to be.

"I don't know. Only if you do."

She had a loveliness about her pale face. But there was something different in her expression. When she talked to him she squinted some, as though she were skeptical of something, as though trying to look past a layer of a fog. Lars wondered why. She swore they would quit climbing after the accident, but Lars had refused. *Been doing it for too damn long,* he had told her. Wasn't going to stop just because of a damned fall. One bad fall.

"I'm fine," he said now.

■■■

When they arrived in Fayetteville, West Virginia, they set up camp and were among the few in the campground. The cold air bled the feeling from Lars's hands, and his fingers felt stiff and false. They ran metal poles through the fabric of their tent, intermittently breathing into cupped hands. The temperature had dropped by nearly twenty degrees. Lars forced the last pole into the metal eye-ring of the tent, which stood up like a pop-up book, and suddenly their portable home for the next two days was ready.

"You want to start the fire and I'll put up the rain fly?" Julie asked.

"You don't need help with the rain fly?"

"No."

"You always need help with the rain fly."

"Since when?"

"Since always."

■ ■ ■

A cricket, trapped between the tent and the rain fly, thudded against taut fabric between hops—thick bodily thuds. They lay in the tent, inside their sleeping bags. Julie on her side, back facing him. Lars held his eyes closed for most of thirty minutes but was far from asleep. He turned and put his hand on her hip and gently rubbed her through the sleeping bag.

She hummed a noise that sounded like what.

"You going to sleep?" he asked.

She hummed a noise that sounded like yes.

"Okay," he said.

■ ■ ■

He woke and cooked breakfast while she stayed in the tent. The campground smelled of the fire, of sticky smoke and hickory. It sank down into the cotton of his clothes and the hair of his arms. He had scrambled eggs for himself, but nothing for her—she being vegan. Her liberal sensibilities had begun to bother him more. Remembering about dairy products. Remembering that honey counted. Remembering to buy the right shoes. He had bought her a pair of climbing shoes one time made with real leather. When her face dropped, he had realized: the vegan thing. She said, using the word sweetie, that she couldn't wear them. He told her that it wasn't like he wanted her to eat the goddamned things.

She came out of her tent with a purple and green beanie on her head—her dark hair sticking out just past her neck.

"Breakfast," he said, holding his plate of scrambled eggs.

"Bagel," she said.

"Chicken embryo," he said. She smiled and gave him the finger.

"Where are we going today?" she asked.

"I want to climb Jesus and Tequila."

"Okay," she said. "You think you're up for it?"

"Why wouldn't I be?" he asked.

"That climb's a 12b. You haven't climbed anything harder than 11 since the accident."

"So?"

"Just wondering if you're in shape to. You might need to pace yourself."

"I'm plenty paced. I'll be fine. I can go bolt to bolt if I have to."

"Okay."

"It'll be fine."

"Okay," she said, letting it go.

■ ■ ■

They climbed down the ladders to the base of the cliffs, negotiating the terrain with their packs full of gear. The rock swirled with reds and oranges. Flakes of stone and boulders scattered the ground from where some seismic activity had probably ripped them from the cliffs millions of years ago. Julie wanted to climb a warm-up first, so they hiked past Jesus and Tequila to a climb called Glass Onion. Five bolts to the anchors. Easy enough.

"What do you think's the heighth here?" she asked.

"What?"

"The heighth. What do you think it is?"

"It's *height*, not heighth. There's no 'h' at the end like there is in width."

"Sorry. Jesus," she said, turning around to pick up an end of the rope. "What do you think the height is here?" putting particular emphasis on the t.

"I don't know," he scratched at the back of his neck and stared at the broken rocks on the ground.

Julie tied the rope in her harness and then climbed with little effort and a dancer-like grace. She pulled a quickdraw from her harness and clipped it to her rope and the first bolt.

The rocks swirled with reds and oranges. Flakes of stone and boulders scattered the ground...

She continued to climb with that precision footwork he taught her, clipping into the next bolt and higher to the next and the next until she reached the top. She called down for him to lower and he did. When she reached the ground and stood under her own weight, she began to untie her knot from her harness.

"How was it?" Lars asked, a question that he asked after nearly every climb.

"Good. Easy warm-up."

"Cool," he said.

Once she was free, she pulled the rope down, walked away from him, and sat on the ground, changing out her climbing shoes for her hiking shoes. Lars picked up an end of the rope and tied into his harness. When Julie was ready, he began climbing, clipping the first bolt and then higher to the next just as she did. At one point in the climb, he considered letting go. Falling. Falling to get the feeling of falling again. To get the thrill and not be afraid. He thought that if he fell—fell big enough—that she'd lower him to the ground and things would revert back to what they had once been. Like an easy fix. Take once daily and all will be well again. All better. But he didn't. The thought made the back of his skull ache, so he kept climbing to the top until he finished and lowered back to the ground without incident.

■ ■ ■

Jesus and Tequila, an *arête,* stood from the ground like the bow of a rusted ship. The bright azure rope was neatly stacked, and Lars tied into his harness and checked the security of his new helmet, trying to divert his thoughts away from what he was about to do and why he was about to do it. He looked at Julie as she picked at calluses in her palm.

"Ready?" he asked.

She looked away from her hand and then to him. "You?"

"I guess so."

"Okay, go do it."

The sun had cooked the rock and the warmth felt nice in the cooler temps. He put the rubber of his right climbing shoe on the rock and brought his weight into the wall and began his ascent. He made the first clip and continued to climb to the next and then the next. Grit and sweat pooled in the creases of his hands and so he reached behind, dipping one hand at a time into his chalk bag. Plumes of chalk left the small cotton bag like clouds of exhaust. He had been on the climb before, so he knew most of the moves. He knew what was coming and knew the places where he'd likely fall. As he approached those places, the sweat in his palms dampened the chalk on his fingers to a paste so that he had to reach behind into the bag again.

Air blew against the rock and the gusts hummed loudly inside his ear. He had climbed nearly sixty feet off the deck. Birds flew in the distance at eye-level, long past the tree line, and he felt exposed. Exposed to the sun and to the rock. He thought of this thing that he did, this sport, this activity. Blood filled his forearms, making it more difficult to open and close his fingers on the features of the rock. He felt the fall coming and tried to fight it. The last time he clipped into the wall was several feet below. The fall would be a long one and there wasn't much he could do about it. He could climb back down but was already exhausted. His legs trembled and he prepared himself. He held on for a while longer to bide his time. During the free fall, Lars would feel the rush. He would feel his intestines push their way into his chest cavity, and in the three-second ride down, he would wonder if he'd eventually slow to a stop before hitting the deck.

He thought about the fall. He thought about her. He thought about the stone and the brutal nature of it. Something to be conquered, something to be afraid of. He'd lost it, that much he knew. The back of his skull stung and he lost all clear thought and focus. He lost it all to the rock, giving in to it. Letting it win. He let go of the rock knowing that at the bottom there would be no reward. That if the rope did in fact bring him safely to the ground, she would stand there, again, and resume picking at the skin of her hands, paying him no mind. There would only be the fall. Not what he once was—instead, a freshly neutered animal lying in a corner, trembling and useless. He fell, holding his hands out in front of him, watching streaks of rock zip by inches from his face, bracing for impact. ■

BLACK DOG

She has pared her life
to essentials.
Heart failing,
each breath taken seriously,
walking is not mandatory
except for brief trips
out the kitchen door
to pee in the snowy garden.
This effort requires
hours of sleep to recover.
Kibble holds no interest;
a chicken breast,
the last chunk of roast beef in gravy,
hand-fed bites of lamb and rice
her due
after faithful years
retrieving anything we threw.
She knows what matters
at the end
and positions herself
near doorways
so her humans
must bow down
to pet her as they pass.
Her sad eyes
say stop,
sit, stay,
and we drop
obedient before her
to stroke her white chin and greying ears,

the weight of all our days
rising and falling, rising and falling
with her chest.

CATHY LENTES

CHRISTMAS
IN AUGUST

JENNIFER BARTON

"I expected more appliqués," I said, scanning the line of extras in front of us. Chad and Lee nodded as they shielded their eyes from the rising sun and wiped sweat from their brows. Both were taller than Carrie and I, and were taking the brunt of the heat.

"Yes, definitely expected more sequins," said Carrie. Since this was going to be a Christmas movie, the production company email had said to wear long pants and winter sweaters, as Christmassy as we could manage, and to bring a coat. Each of us had done that, along with the couple hundred people around us. The email hadn't mentioned the long wait outside in the sun, however, and everyone's fancy—but mostly unsparkly—winter clothes were now showing rings of sweat.

The four of us had straggled in together on a tram from Dollywood's parking lot to the main gate, and hit it off quickly. When you meet other people who are able to leave their jobs and families on a random Friday in August just to be an extra in a Dolly Parton Christmas movie, it isn't hard to find things to talk about. Originally a friend from Knoxville was supposed to come with me, but he'd bailed at the last minute, so I was here alone. On the forty-five minute drive from Knoxville down to Pigeon Forge, I'd wondered if I would find anyone to talk to, or if I'd have fun doing this by myself, but filming hadn't even started and I already felt like I'd found my tribe. Many of the people in line around us were older, possibly retirees, but the four of us were in our thirties and had loved Dolly for most of our lives. Not much explanation was needed amongst us—the love we shared for her talent, her generosity, and her acceptance and love for all people erased the usual getting-to-know-you conversation gaps.

"Wonder who those people are over there?" I nodded toward a shorter line across the asphalt from us. There were a couple of tree planters between our line and theirs, and they were receiving most of the shade. "Are they more special than us or something?"

"I think they're the ones who were here yesterday," Chad said. This was surprising—the movie company had said the other filming day would be Saturday, not Thursday, but Lee said someone reported on a Dolly fan site that the date had been changed. This meant we wouldn't be the first extras to be filmed, and that the people in the shorter line would probably be put in the front rows so they'd match up with whatever footage was shot yesterday. Our dreams of pointing ourselves out to friends and family on our TV screens began to fade, but we were still going to spend the day with Dolly, so who cared if we didn't get close-ups?

"And I don't know if it's true or not," Chad said, "but they said Dolly wasn't on set yesterday." Carrie and I squinted up at him, concerned about more than just the heat now. The movie company's description of the project said she would be here and each of us had made sacrifices based on that. Chad and Lee had taken time off from their jobs in Morristown, Tennessee, and Carrie had taken off work, left her husband and kids for the weekend, and driven down from Ohio. The community college where I work wasn't back in session yet, so I didn't have to take off, but I had arranged for my husband to come home early to let our dogs out. If Dolly didn't show, we'd all be crushed. This was probably our one and only chance to be something more than Dolly fans—it was our chance to perform with her, in however small a fashion.

"But the email said she'd be here," I said. In my voice I could almost hear the six-year-old me who'd cried when my parents wouldn't take me to see Dolly at the local civic center. Of course that was a reasonable response from them—what normal six-year-old would even know Dolly was playing nearby, let alone cry to go see her? But I was an only child and also adopted, so at some point before memory, I'd latched onto Dolly as something like a favorite aunt and loved her as fiercely as if she were a blood relation. Even before I knew what the words in her songs meant, her big smile and friendly voice meant pure, uncomplicated joy to me. And here I was thirty years later, still needing that heart connection with a stranger who felt like kin.

"I saw her being interviewed here on the news last night," I said, "so she must be around somewhere. She has an apartment in Dollywood, right?"

"She used to," Chad said. "I think she stays somewhere in Splash Country now."

"It was above Applejack's restaurant, across from the replica of the cabin she grew up in," Carrie added. "There's a staircase up to it and it's got a pink roof."

"There are pictures online of the rooms," Lee said. "It's just what you'd imagine it'd look like. Really pink and frilly, kind of like a Barbie house."

For the first time in my life I was outmatched in Dolly fandom. And it was the really Dolly behind the glitz...that I wanted to know.

I switched my coat to my less sweaty arm and didn't ask any more questions. Even though I had been a Dolly fan for as long as I could remember—I had rented *9 to 5* over and over again when my family got a VCR in the mid-eighties, read her autobiography twice, bought her albums and went to see her in concert whenever I could—for the first time in my life I was outmatched in Dolly fandom. And it was the real Dolly behind the glitz, or in this case, the real Dolly apartment behind the Dollywood version of her childhood home, that I wanted to know.

Our passion for Dolly was equal, though, and although we joked about the fans who would camp outside Dolly's house or fill their entire houses with her memorabilia, none of us laughed too hard. After all, what had drawn us here? Surely it wasn't just the chance to be onscreen in a crowd, where we probably weren't even going to be able to find ourselves later. And it was more than just brushing shoulders with a celebrity, since all four of us, and probably most of the other people in line, had seen Dolly on multiple occasions. We didn't discuss it directly, but I think it was that for a few hours we would be part of Dolly's life and she would be part of ours. She would be playing Dolly Parton in a staged, country music American Idol-type show, we would be playing the audience members, and together we would be creating something, not just witnessing a performance. That is, if she showed up.

"She'd better be here," Carrie said. "That's all I have to say."

A skeletal wardrobe lady with a thick French accent came down the line, eyeing everyone's outfits and making people even more irritable by telling those with shirt sleeves rolled up or sweaters removed to replace them when they went inside. When she was done, the line finally started to move. Since we were near the end, though, we still had a while to bake in the sun. Dollywood patrons were starting to arrive, some of whom stood in our line until someone realized they weren't in winter clothes and directed them to the ticket windows. Eventually we made it to a table where we signed release forms and were shown to the back door of a theater. Our long, hot wait slipped into memory when we stepped into air conditioning and were greeted with all the hallmarks of a movie set—folding tables spread with cookies and crackers, thick electric cables taped to the floor, barn-doored lights affixed to sandbagged stands, and lots of people with badges around their necks moving quickly and having intense conversations about sightlines and camera angles.

"We're here!" I said as we climbed up the theater's side steps to find seats.

"Finally." Chad moved aside so Carrie and I could slide down an empty row.

"Now let's just hope Dolly is too," Carrie said.

Our row was in the middle right of the theater, almost directly in line with the sound booth. The theater was big, but not huge—about 500 seats, so we had a clear view of the stage. It was decorated with Christmas trees and set up with microphones, a drum set and guitars. No musicians or actors were out yet, just crew members hustling to get cameras set up and the lighting just right. Things looked promising, though. Surely some kind of musical performance was going to take place, so at least we wouldn't have to cheer at nothing.

While we waited, we compared how many times we'd seen Dolly perform and whether or not we'd met her—Carrie had at a book signing and I had at a record signing. We'd all seen Dolly live numerous times, but while I enjoyed her concerts, something about them always left me a little empty. Not that she wasn't wonderful, because she always was—warm and funny and tremendously talented—but her shows were so carefully scripted that it was like watching a Vegas act. Once I saw her twice on the same tour, and except for a few bits of stage banter, the shows were exactly the same, from songs to jokes to outfits. I wanted something different, something Dolly would probably never do because she wouldn't be "Dolly" if she did. I wanted something stripped-down, unscripted, and intimate. I wanted to hear old songs she never played anymore, played on her own guitar. I wanted to feel like the performance was as special to her as it was to me, and not just another night of The Dolly Parton Show.

By ten thirty, all of the extras were seated in the theater and things were starting to look ready with the crew. The band members were tuning their instruments onstage and a dolly-mounted camera behind them was doing practice runs, rolling back and forth. A middle-aged lady with white-blonde hair and a baggy red dress had been called to the center microphone to do lighting and camera tests, but still there was no sign of Dolly. Clearly this woman was a Dolly stand-in, but was the actual Dolly here, too? There was still no word or sign until one of the crew member's radio blared, "Dolly's on her way to set, one minute." Crew members scrambled onstage and the four of us looked at each other, eyes wide, before scanning the theater to find where she might enter.

Suddenly Carrie grabbed my arm and pointed toward the entrance we'd used half an hour ago. All heads in the audience turned toward a flock of people circling a figure in a red sparkly dress with big blonde hair. The whole group disappeared quickly up the stairs behind the stage and I wasn't able to see the face of the central figure, but there was no mistaking who it was. Dolly was here. Would she be on set for half an hour or all day? There was no telling, but for the first time that day, we knew our efforts to be here would be rewarded.

Soon after Dolly's arrival, her stand-in left the stage and things started moving faster than they had so far that morning. An assistant snapped the clapboard in front of one of the cameras, the director called "Action!", and a stage manager made the announcement we'd been waiting and hoping for: "Ladies and gentlemen, please welcome your host of Country Star of Tomorrow, our national treasure, Ms. Dolly Parton!"

Carrie, Chad, Lee, and I leapt to our feet, along with the rest of the audience. Dolly waved and smiled as she made her way to the microphone and took up her guitar. Her sparkly red dress was almost electric under the stage lights.

"Merry Christmas, everybody!" she said. "Nothing gets me in the Christmas spirit more than a good old Christmas song, so what do you say we sing one together?"

Everybody cheered and she and the band launched into "Jingle Bells." Chad, Lee, Carrie and I clapped and sang along with the rest of the audience and other than the fact we were singing a Christmas song in August, it felt and looked like every other Dolly Parton performance I'd seen. Her hair and makeup were lacquered in place, her lines and lyrics were scrolling on a huge teleprompter by the sound booth, and the band was playing flawlessly, until…a sour note sounded and the music stopped. We held our hands apart in mid-clap.

"Shoot!" Dolly said in the silence. "How could I screw up 'Jingle Bells?" The audience laughed and she looked to the director at the side of the stage. "Can we do it again?" He nodded and she turned back to the audience. "How y'all doing, by the way?"

We all cheered again, even more wildly than we had when she first came onstage. She was talking to us, and not in the way a performer will ask an audience how it's doing, just to get applause and keep the energy up. She spoke in a quick, down-to-business way, like a team leader addressing her team. We ended up singing along to "Jingle Bells" four more times

Her hair and makeup were lacquered in place, her lines and lyrics were scrolling on a huge teleprompter by the sound booth, and the band was playing flawlessly...

because she kept snagging on one spot in the song, and by the end of it, we were truly acting. None of us wanted to hear "Jingle Bells" again anytime soon, even if it was Dolly singing it.

She moved to the side of the stage so the crew could change the camera angles and extras began calling out, "Dolly, I love you!" from the darkened theater. She was talking to people in the wings, but had taken her microphone with her and spoke into it: "I know what you want me to say…" Everyone waited, and I wondered if we were about to see a side of Dolly we'd never seen before, maybe one we didn't want to see. When we were paying to see her perform, she had an obligation to tolerate gushing from the audience, but she had no such duty today. She put a hand on her hip, pursed her lips and said, "Go wait in the truck!" Everyone laughed—this was her go-to joke when someone said they loved her during a concert, and all of us had probably heard it as many times as we'd seen her perform.

Since the door was open to shouting "I love yous", though, some extras began shouting requests for other things, like pictures and hugs and signatures on their body parts to later be tattooed. Dolly graciously declined each request, saying that if she started that, we wouldn't get any filming done, but that didn't stop the outbursts. Each time one happened, Carrie, Chad, Lee, and I would roll our eyes or shout-whisper "Shut up!" The four of us were lumped in with the whole, after all, and we didn't want Dolly to be annoyed with us.

"She just said she wasn't going to do pictures!" Carrie said after another loud request. "Why do people react to her like that?"

Chad and Lee shrugged their shoulders, but I thought about this, and about my own reasons for being here. Just like the super-fans, I wanted my own piece of Dolly, but the piece I wanted wasn't as tangible as a picture with her or a signature on my butt or shoulder. I still wanted something, though—a shared experience with her, some kind of genuine connection—and somehow, like the people who were yelling around us, I felt like I could have it.

"I think it's because she's all love," I said. "Everyone wants some of it, and since she doesn't shut anyone out, maybe they feel entitled to it." They, I thought. Us. Me.

Carrie nodded. "I think maybe you're on to something."

The next few scenes involved the actors who were playing finalists in the Country Star of Tomorrow contest, whom Dolly introduced and chatted with before leaving them to perform their songs. She would chat with crew members and actors in the wings between takes, and I wondered what they were talking about—how does one make small talk with Dolly Parton?—but she always had her microphone with her and whenever someone in the audience yelled something out to her, she would always respond.

"I'm so glad I got to see you today!" a lady near the front said to Dolly at one point. "I've never seen anyone famous before."

"Well I'm glad I'm famous so you can say you saw me," Dolly said. People's laughter drowned out the lady's response, but Dolly nodded along to whatever she was saying and then said into the mic, "Well say hello to your mom for me."

Chad, Lee, Carrie, and I looked down the row at each other. It was like one of our own relations had just said something embarrassing, but of course Dolly was okay with it. Of course she'd want the lady to say hello to her mother for her.

The first hour of filming stretched into many, and if not for Dolly's increasingly frequent chat sessions with the audience and short breaks into song, the boredom would've been insufferable. "She's ruined the filmmaking experience for me," Carrie told us when we broke for a lunch of cheese cubes, crackers, and vegetables with dip. "I could never last this long on another set without Dolly there to entertain me."

We worried that Dolly wouldn't return after the break—we were tired, but she had to be more tired than us after standing, talking, and singing most of the day—but not long after we were all back in our seats, Dolly was back, too. She cheerfully answered audience questions while the camera crew moved the dolly to the back of the theater, and if she was tired, she didn't show it. The crew also moved several extras to fill seats that would be in the shots and my friends and I ended up in the middle center of the theater, with the dolly crew directly behind us. At first they talked shop as they set up the track and mounted the camera, but when Dolly began humming the opening bars of "Little Sparrow," the camera operator said to his crewman, "You know, she can't not entertain. Have you noticed that?"

"Uh-huh," the guy grunted. He was pushing the camera down the aisle to practice their shot.

"If she has an audience, she can't ignore them. She just has to entertain."

Carrie and I glanced at each other—the crewmen didn't know we were listening, so they might say anything. We were about to hear what Dolly was really like, and not just what she or her publicity managers wanted to be known.

"She's so genuine, though," the cameraman continued. "It's not like she's faking it. And professional—I've waited hours for

We were about to hear what Dolly was really like, and not just what she or her publicity managers wanted to be known.

actresses to come out of their trailers after the shot is ready, but Dolly is always here when she's supposed to be, and she knows her stuff."

After the camera rolled past, Carrie and I exchanged quick, joyous smiles. Everything we wanted to be true about Dolly was true, verified by impartial professionals.

We broke around five that evening, when the production company had said we would, but there was still more filming to be done, so the stage manager told the audience that whoever came back after an hour's break would be included in a raffle of signed movie posters, badges, and Dollywood merchandise. I didn't care much about the raffle, but he assured us Dolly would be back, too, so I couldn't leave. The whole day had been special, but I still felt like something was missing, like that one special moment I had come for had not yet happened. Or maybe it had happened and I hadn't recognized it—maybe the whole day was the special moment and I just wasn't seeing it in a large enough scope. Either way, I had to stay and see.

The hot afternoon sun was jarring after spending so many dark hours in air-conditioned Christmastime. Outside in the real world, though, or at least in the real Dollywood world, it was still late summer and the four of us began sweating again soon after we exited the theater. We circled up away from the crowd, blinking fast in the sudden brightness.

"You guys staying?" Chad asked.

I knew my answer, but eyed the others and wondered if anyone had had enough, if a few more hours of the same stuff we'd seen all day would just be too much. Maybe they thought to stay would be to enter into full-on crazy fandom. Even so, I couldn't leave and perhaps miss what I'd come for. I nodded and glanced at Carrie, who also nodded. Whew, I thought. At least I'm not the only one.

"Are you?" I asked the guys.

They nodded as well. "We've stayed this long," Chad said. "We might as well stay till the end."

We headed off into Dollywood to stretch our stiff legs and again I was glad to have run into this group, to not have to explain why I didn't want to leave or beg someone I'd brought to stay. We spent our break walking through Craftsman's Valley, where a new roller coaster plunged behind a working leathersmith, blacksmith, carriage maker, and across from a one-room chapel named after the doctor who delivered Dolly. Split rail fences and log structures dotted the carefully manicured lawns and flower gardens, creating a postcard-ready version of the grittier Appalachia I knew as a kid in southwest Virginia, and knew now as an adult in Knoxville. In nearby counties, extreme poverty, drug epidemics, and barren land ravaged by the coal industry might belie this Appalachian fantasyland, but even for all of Dollywood's calculation and polish, its spirit felt genuine.

After all, the aspects of Appalachian culture on display around us were the same as those Dolly had always honored in her songs, strains of which we heard as we passed by gift shops and waiting areas for rides. Many Appalachian families were and still are just as hard-working, resourceful, and devoted to each other as Dolly's, and her most personal songs have always testified to that. Songs such as "Smoky Mountain Memories," "My Tennessee Mountain Home," and "In the Good Old Days (When Times Were Bad)" shine a positive light on a region that is so often depicted as backward and deprived in the national press. Her masterwork, "Coat of Many Colors," tells the story of growing up poor and learning that her mother's love and care made Dolly far richer than money ever could. Ironically, that song helped Dolly become the multi-millionaire she is today, and even though she's a long way from being a poor little girl in a coat made of vibrant rags, she's clearly still living the song's message. Dollywood creates a multitude of jobs for people in Dolly's home county, preserves regional traditions by employing local craftspeople, and contributes revenue to her children's literacy program. Without it, Sevier County, Tennessee, could very well be in the same situation as my home county—Pulaski County, Virginia was decimated by the almost-total loss of industry and is now ranked as one of the state's poorest locations.

Now, after spending most of the day in the presence of Dolly herself, I could see how much Dollywood mirrored her. There was real caring and heritage embedded within the rusticity, so rather than seeming hokey or contrived, the park's gleam and its throwbacks to a bygone Appalachia imparted the same respect and dignity that Dolly's songs about the region do. The variety of accents in the park visitors around us, and even amongst the four of us, proved that Dolly was something of an Appalachian ambassador. Her charm stretched far beyond east Tennessee and made Dollywood more meaningful than one might expect a Dolly Parton-themed amusement park to be. But as Dolly has often said about herself, "There's a heart beneath the boobs and a brain beneath the wig." Clearly that was part of what drew me and people from everywhere to her.

We returned to the theater just as an oncoming thunderstorm was shutting down rides and sending most of Dollywood's patrons out of the gates. The remaining scenes to be filmed turned out to mostly be close-ups, though, which didn't even require the audience to be seen or heard. For a few shots, the director even had us pretend-clap. It did help keep us alert, but tiredness and a growing sense of uselessness were crumpling our spirits. If Dolly hadn't continued her jokes and banter, I'm sure the four of us would've walked out.

Her people. She'd enfolded us, like a line had been drawn and she'd ushered us close.

By eight o'clock, we were approaching what had to be the final shots. The crew had filmed the same scenes over and over throughout the day from every imaginable angle, and there didn't seem to be one spot in the theater they hadn't covered. Dolly was on stage to film the finale of the Country Star of Tomorrow show, and while the crew got ready, she talked to the audience and director about old country songs, and sang snatches of a few of them. He was trying to learn all about country music in one day, she said, and everyone laughed. Earlier he'd tried to ask the audience Dolly trivia questions, such as which movie she'd made with Lily Tomlin, but this hadn't gone over well. Even most non-Dolly fans would know that was *9 to 5* and when the audience's groaning subsided, Dolly asked him,

"Who do you think these people are? These are my people!"

Her people. She'd enfolded us, like a line had been drawn and she'd ushered us close. Even though Dolly was on stage and both a literal and figurative gulf existed between us and her, she was on our side and the director and the rest of the crew and actors were on the other. While they could talk to her one-on-one and knew her as a professional, we knew her life, music, and career from the start until now, and she knew we knew it. We were the audience she had known most of her life, the people she'd imagined when she sang into a tin can on a broom handle on her parents' front porch. Our relationship went way back, even before some of us were born, while the crew would mostly know her for the length of the shoot.

The director's interest in the music seemed genuine, though, and after a chat about Hank Williams, someone in the audience yelled out, "Tennessee Waltz!"

"Who did that one?" the director asked Dolly.

"Oh shoot," Dolly said. "I would've told you if you hadn't asked." She thought for a minute and then someone in the audience yelled out, "Patti Page!"

"Patti Page, that's right," she said. "I knew that one, I really did. That's a hard one to sing—you start way down low and end way up high." She turned to the band, though, and hummed a few bars. They strummed softly and she sang the opening line over the murmurs of the audience and of the director and actors joking around onstage. Just a few bars into the song, however, a hush fell over the theater and even the crew members who were setting up the next shot stopped what they were doing to watch and listen.

"But I remember the night and the Tennessee Waltz," she sang, her voice rising and falling, sounding both strong and fragile. She took a step toward center stage and everyone seemed to become simultaneously aware that we were in the presence of something rare and beautiful and even a bit unearthly. "Only God knows how much I have lost..." She continued her climb up to the chorus that tells of losing a love to a friend. Her voice took each heart in the room in its trembling embrace and if I had been able to think anything at all, I would've known this was it. This was what I had come for, what I had wanted from Dolly for all those years. For a brief, unplanned moment, we were all united and elevated not just by Dolly's talent, but by the genuine, unguarded love that poured past the wig and boobs and make-up on the vessel of her voice.

Thunderous applause erupted before she could get the last note out and the stage manager said into his microphone, "Our national treasure, Ms. Dolly Parton!" He wasn't acting this time, as he had been when he first introduced her that morning. The director came over and kissed Dolly's hand. Dolly took a bow, and after a few more short takes, our twelve-hour workday was over. She left the stage as soon as her scenes were done, headed for a bus that would take her back to Nashville. We waited for the raffle, where Lee won a hat and shirt, and then the four of us carried our coats out into the warm night. We shared a round of hugs before heading back into our lives, more like old friends than one-day acquaintances, forever tied now by our deepened love of Dolly. I started the car and cued up Dolly's "Here You Come Again" on my iPod. It wasn't "Tennessee Waltz," which to my knowledge she'd never recorded, but still the soulful quaver in her voice made my skin feel electric, just as it had in the theater. Christmas had indeed come early this year. ■

VIDUITY FROM A ROOFTOP

New beasts in the blue
full-lipped morning.

Ground flower, star-glass,
and a seemingly rocking pasture.

Did she sleep?

Slant brown hills. Covered bridge.
Colors feather village houses,

an instrumental passage
of scarlet weeks gone by quickly.

But the strange slowness of days
cradle an image of her frowning.

These doors of passion
are impractical,

a filmic fire, robes stained
with flesh oil

and bubbling smoke
from a falling building's dust.

The future is the speck of a bird
barely seen from the peripheral,

a world of broken pictures
fluidly level.

Wake lost, walk,
always to wonder

if the young widow slept
with murder all around her.

TERRELL JAMAL TERRY

SCYTHE

Across steel wastelands
and graffiti faux life,
abandonment on the low.

Few lilies or fruit trees,
but the sky hasn't died
over captivity

in a cultural desert. Layers
of years reappearing.
Some see newness, yet

you wear them as a wardrobe
worn in. Miles of space,
the city not there and not gone.

From a phobia of touching curses—
hands glove yellowed maps.
A trail of staggered homes survived,

one shelters your youngest niece
who blows kisses through
civilized delusion, first duties

before bus stations, unintentional
dystopian museums.
There might be very few things

that are beautifully destroyed.
Where can you live
and still feel alive? Dare, anywhere.

TERRELL JAMAL TERRY

BOOK REVIEWS

Jane Hicks. *Driving with the Dead*. Lexington, Ky.: The University Press of Kentucky, 2014. 82 pages. Softcover. $19.95.

Reviewed by Erin Keane

In *Driving With the Dead*, poet Jane Hicks's stunning follow-up to her 2005 debut collection *Blood and Bone Remember* (winner of the 2006 Appalachian Book of the Year), Hicks turns her rigorous eye toward the poet's work: "the naming of what matters." As the title promises, the poems in *Driving With the Dead* are poems of loss, but Hicks has no time for maudlin remembrances, for the soft, idle elegies of the sated. Instead, Hicks settles her unflinching eye on what truly matters to her—on rural cemeteries and their specific rituals, on the unraveling of marriages and of innocence, on the dead and what we owe them—with a ferocity and wit that are wholly her own.

In "The Color of Loss," an *ars poetica* for this collection, Hicks names an understanding of grief that is hidden yet steely, both "blackberries stored in / dark cellars" and "the shadowed eyes of the twin / who stares long into the night and waits / for his still half to speak." But this birthright, grief, isn't an indulgence for the poet to coddle. In the concise and determined "A Poet's Work," which she dedicates to a three-year-old boy killed by a strip-mine boulder that crashed the side of Black Mountain into the boy's bedroom, Hicks lays out her demands for herself and her fellow poets: "Spare me the postmodern pout / about dog piss in the gray snow / near the subway entrance" she warns, directing their attention instead to "meth labs that spring up in our rural / gardens" and "mountaintops removed, laid low by greed, / hollows filled, wells poisoned, God's majesty / flattened, fit only for Wal-Mart, the new Ground Zero." Here are the fruits of "judicial disregard," she writes, face them, travel her "ruined roads, moonscape mountains, failed farms" and confront just "how the law measures a baby's life." (Spoiler: as worth "less than the price / of a good pickup truck"—ponder that, academic poets preoccupied with the quality of light in a Tuscan monastery.)

In another poem for the same boy, the loose sonnet "Black Mountain Breakdown," Hicks offers a more direct elegy for the dead child. "Things rest / as we left them," Hicks writes, in a precise explication of grief and its lingering effects, which are also made clear in Hicks' poems about how survivors in rural communities bear the generational wounds of war.

In "Draft Lottery," Hicks takes the reader back to 1970, inside a small town's Taco King, where a group of terrified teenage employees watch the broadcast on the office TV, waiting to find out the sum of the afternoon's reaping: "Number 22, Dennis out of school, out of options, / slid to the floor." Hicks turns her grief for the Vietnam generation's collective loss outward, too. In "Expatriate," a soldier in World War II never leaves Normandy, his son and wife at home in the U.S. without a nearby grave to tend, only a telegram and "a photo of his seaside / home, manicured and maintained / by French hosts in gratitude for duty." In "A Poet's Work," she calls attention to a contemporary "child who sobs silently, / her mama a nurse in the Guard, called up, / goodnights a webcam image from Basra."

Cemeteries appear frequently in this book, of course, but they're never commonplace, and are often riddled with unsettling images...

Cemeteries appear frequently in this book, of course, but they're never commonplace, and are often riddled with unsettling images—the "Beanie bears, balloons, pinwheels, / little lambs" littering the graves of children in "Kindergarten," the ritual of homecoming picnics spread out in a rural cemetery where, distracted by a gaggle of balloons and a card meant to trace their flight, the speaker stubs her toe on the gravestone of an old boyfriend who died in Vietnam. "I retrieve the balloon card from my pocket and drive / toward the post office drop box to obey / the careful crayon message: send me back." Throughout the collection, Hicks demonstrates that there is more than one way to tend a grave.

In a daring examination of an unraveling marriage, Hicks writes about a mother, children married (now divorcing themselves) and gone, loading up "the packrat plunder" of the speaker's father into his boat so he could haul his George Wallace stickers and "the black book he believed secret" away. The image of "his Ku Klux Klan hood perched / like a jaunty cap on the motor" is shocking and funny, the mother blaring Marty Robbins until he takes off with his boat trailer, "strewing / dusty propaganda in its wake." In an act of poetic generosity, Hicks offers this darkly humorous and rebellious act of rejecting old, damaging attitudes toward women and minorities to her mother's generation, not to her own.

And Hicks continues throughout the book to deftly subvert expectations of poems about rural life, especially those with deceptively cuddly titles like "Cousins" and "Domestic Arts," abstaining from easy sentiment and embracing more prickly, memorable tales. Those domestic arts? A handed-down tradition of dismantling all but the barest seams of a straying husband's clothes, so his first vigorous move when stepping out would render him naked, as humiliated as a scorned wife. Hicks ends this poem with a warning characteristic of her sly, barbed wit:

Stay close, beloved. I inherited
Mam's sewing box, handed down
by a family of women
big on tradition.

Nestled among the elegies and poems of witness are a few reprieves. Even as she accepts as her enterprise to name the destruction that matters in "A Poet's Work," Hicks offers an answer poem early in the collection to ground the reader. Is "What Matters," with its litany of sensory and natural wonders, meant to lend us solace within all of this grief? The poem comes early in the collection, its welcome cleansing breath of "Rusty dogwoods, flames of maple, / cider clean and bright on the tongue," suggesting yes. ■

Morris Allen Grubbs and Mary Ellen Miller, Eds. *Every Leaf a Mirror: A Jim Wayne Miller Reader.* Lexington, Ky.: The University Press of Kentucky, 2014. 256 pages. Softcover. $30.00.

Reviewed by Nicholas Smith

Every Leaf a Mirror: A Jim Wayne Miller Reader is a collection of poetry, fiction and nonfiction that draws from Miller's accumulated work over decades of artistic and scholarly endeavor. Skillful editing by Morris Grubbs, writer and assistant dean in the Graduate School at the University of Kentucky, and Mary Ellen Miller, the subject's widow and a poet in her own right, places the power of Jim Wayne Miller's writing on full display.

Like many of his contemporaries in Appalachian literature, Miller had humble beginnings. Raised in the mountains of North Carolina, he grew up not knowing he lived less than fifty miles from the homeplaces of literary luminaries like Fred Chappell, Thomas Wolfe, and Wilma Dykeman. Like that of these writers before him, Miller's work often focused on the notion of how people cope with the changing world and the underlying questions of what we hang on to, what we leave behind.

This reader highlights those themes in a triad of sections divided by genre. The first, devoted to Miller's poetry, is subdivided, with each portion exploring a different aspect of his poetic themes and showcasing the range of his thought and craft, including free verse and formed poems with language as fresh as newfound words.

The middle of the poetry section is devoted to Miller's masterwork, "The Brier Sermon". A free verse that blends styles of epic poetry with fable to achieve a parable quality, "The Brier Sermon" has itself taken on a legendary status in the Appalachian literary community. From a busy sidewalk we see the Brier use episodes including a little boy lost far from home and a hunter who walked over a cliff in an effort to urge passersby to reconsider their notion of place and belonging. He speaks freely to the changing crowd, nettling them over environmental degradation and forgetfulness of their roots while simultaneously goading them to expand their way of thinking from the old "ridge to ridge" view into a more global perspective. This candid tone is the culmination of Miller's poetic voice and lends a raw power to the message of his sermon. The Brier convinces us that we "must be born again," and more important, that our rebirth is not only possible but essential, inevitable. We can hang on, he says, like the scared hunter who has fallen over a cliff, or we can let go and be free, choose to return to known earth.

The next section of the anthology is devoted to fiction, drawn from two novels and three short stories. Although by no means weak, this is the lesser of the three sections. The language is evocative and heavy with poetic image. Here we see most clearly reflected Miller's abiding love and understanding of a people and place which arises only after considerable discord between a vanishing way of life and the double threat of increasing globalization and environmental destruction. Always we find ourselves returning to the theme of memory, the conflict of choosing what we will keep and what we will relinquish.

Despite Miller's work being centered on belonging to a particular place, his fiction is reminiscent of immigrant stories in that even in familiar environments the characters often feel a sense of displacement. In the excerpt of "His First Best Country" we see Professor Wells—as a prosaic Brier—struggle with his own homecoming and unable to reconstruct his remembered self. He then takes to the road, and through encounters in real world places such as the Highlander Center in the mountains of Tennessee, Wells develops his perspective on what it means to be both intimate with, and simultaneously divorced from, a home.

The anthology's last section is its gem. In these essays and interview with Appalachian scholar Loyal Jones, we see Miller revealed in his final form, a vicar for the knowledge of what it means to be an Appalachian in both practical and poetic terms. The attentive reader will find himself flipping back again and again to the fiction and poetry as Miller rapidly expands each aspect of his writing into synecdoche, that in which the part represents the whole. We begin to get a sense of how inclusive and interconnected a vision Miller possessed—one that proves he understood Appalachia from the inside out. Miller was what co-editor Mary Ellen Miller called "a farmboy turned academic." From the keen—and often agonizing—grief and love that characterize his creative work to his clairvoyant scholarship on the Appalachian people and their roots as a region of immigrants, Miller's struggle to grasp his own history and place allowed him to accurately assess the present and keep a perceptive eye on the future.

Finally, Miller's work is framed by three excellent essays by Mary Ellen Miller, Appalachian historian Ron Eller, and bestselling novelist Silas House. Here we get a glimpse of the impact of Miller's work on his community of Appalachian readers and writers. His widow, Mary Ellen, provides an intimate but unflinching view of his life. House lets us in on what it means to be a young Appalachian discovering Miller's work and feeling its impact for the first time. Eller places Miller into historical context as the everyman turned intellectual. Each contributor writes from a perspective that neatly parallels the sections of this reader, both contextualizing and enriching the text.

Every Leaf a Mirror calls us to bear witness to the urgency of Miller's writing. He reminds us that we are Briers all, immigrants remembering our first countries, as he transports us through his Appalachia like a mountain-born Joyce. Buy this book, read it with a pencil in hand, talk back to it. Stand in the word rows with the sun at your back. ■

UNITED STATES POSTAL SERVICE®

Statement of Ownership, Management, and Circulation (All Periodicals Publications Except Requester Publications)

1. Publication Title	2. Publication Number	3. Filing Date
Appalachian Heritage	0 3 6 3 – 2 8 1 8	September 26, 2014
4. Issue Frequency	5. Number of Issues Published Annually	6. Annual Subscription Price
quarterly (Winter, Spring, Summer, Fall)	4	$30 individuals $40 institutions

7. Complete Mailing Address of Known Office of Publication *(Not printer) (Street, city, county, state, and ZIP+4®)*

Loyal Jones Appalachian Center, CPO Box 2166,
Berea College, Madison County, Berea, KY 40404

Contact Person: Suzi Waters

Telephone *(Include area code)*: 919-962-4201

8. Complete Mailing Address of Headquarters or General Business Office of Publisher *(Not printer)*

The University of North Carolina Press, 116 South Boundary Street, Chapel Hill, Orange County, NC 27514

9. Full Names and Complete Mailing Addresses of Publisher, Editor, and Managing Editor *(Do not leave blank)*

Publisher *(Name and complete mailing address)*

The University of North Carolina Press, 116 South Boundary Street, Chapel Hill, Orange County, NC 27514

Editor *(Name and complete mailing address)*

Jason K. Howard, Loyal Jones Appalachian Center, CPO Box 2166, Berea College, Madison County, Berea, KY 40404

Managing Editor *(Name and complete mailing address)*

Same as above editor

10. Owner *(Do not leave blank. If the publication is owned by a corporation, give the name and address of the corporation immediately followed by the names and addresses of all stockholders owning or holding 1 percent or more of the total amount of stock. If not owned by a corporation, give the names and addresses of the individual owners. If owned by a partnership or other unincorporated firm, give its name and address as well as those of each individual owner. If the publication is published by a nonprofit organization, give its name and address.)*

Full Name	Complete Mailing Address
Loyal Jones Appalachian Center	CPO Box 2166, 205 North Main Street, Berea, KY 40404

11. Known Bondholders, Mortgagees, and Other Security Holders Owning or Holding 1 Percent or More of Total Amount of Bonds, Mortgages, or Other Securities. If none, check box ——► ☑ None

Full Name	Complete Mailing Address

12. Tax Status *(For completion by nonprofit organizations authorized to mail at nonprofit rates) (Check one)*
The purpose, function, and nonprofit status of this organization and the exempt status for federal income tax purposes:

☑ Has Not Changed During Preceding 12 Months

☐ Has Changed During Preceding 12 Months *(Publisher must submit explanation of change with this statement)*

PS Form **3526**, July 2014 *[Page 1 of 4 (see instructions page 4)]* PSN: 7530-01-000-9931 **PRIVACY NOTICE:** See our privacy policy on *www.usps.com*.

13. Publication Title	14. Issue Date for Circulation Data Below	
Appalachian Heritage	Summer 2014, 42#3, September 18, 2014	
15. Extent and Nature of Circulation	**Average No. Copies Each Issue During Preceding 12 Months**	**No. Copies of Single Issue Published Nearest to Filing Date**
a. Total Number of Copies *(Net press run)*	1000	1000
b. Paid Circulation *(By Mail and Outside the Mail)* (1) Mailed Outside-County Paid Subscriptions Stated on PS Form 3541 (Include paid distribution above nominal rate, advertiser's proof copies, and exchange copies)	404	396
(2) Mailed In-County Paid Subscriptions Stated on PS Form 3541 *(Include paid distribution above nominal rate, advertiser's proof copies, and exchange copies)*		
(3) Paid Distribution Outside the Mails Including Sales Through Dealers and Carriers, Street Vendors, Counter Sales, and Other Paid Distribution Outside USPS®		
(4) Paid Distribution by Other Classes of Mail Through the USPS (e.g., First-Class Mail®)		
c. Total Paid Distribution *[Sum of 15b (1), (2), (3), and (4)]* ▶	404	396
d. Free or Nominal Rate Distribution *(By Mail and Outside the Mail)* (1) Free or Nominal Rate Outside-County Copies included on PS Form 3541	77	80
(2) Free or Nominal Rate In-County Copies Included on PS Form 3541		
(3) Free or Nominal Rate Copies Mailed at Other Classes Through the USPS (e.g., First-Class Mail)		
(4) Free or Nominal Rate Distribution Outside the Mail *(Carriers or other means)*		
e. Total Free or Nominal Rate Distribution *(Sum of 15d (1), (2), (3) and (4))*	77	80
f. Total Distribution *(Sum of 15c and 15e)* ▶	481	476
g. Copies not Distributed *(See Instructions to Publishers #4 (page #3))* ▶	519	524
h. Total *(Sum of 15f and g)*	1000	1000
i. Percent Paid *(15c divided by 15f times 100)* ▶	84%	83%

* If you are claiming electronic copies, go to line 16 on page 3. If you are not claiming electronic copies, skip to line 17 on page 3.

17. Publication of Statement of Ownership

☒ If the publication is a general publication, publication of this statement is required. Will be printed in the Winter 2015 issue of this publication.

☐ Publication not required.

18. Signature and Title of Editor, Publisher, Business Manager, or Owner

Robert Dreher [signature] CFO, UNC PRESS

Date 9/25/2014

I certify that all information furnished on this form is true and complete. I understand that anyone who furnishes false or misleading information on this form or who omits material or information requested on the form may be subject to criminal sanctions (including fines and imprisonment) and/or civil sanctions (including civil penalties).

PS Form **3526**, July 2014

CONTRIBUTORS

Laurie Albin is currently earning her MFA from Arizona State University in Tempe, Arizona, where she spends her afternoons listening to Elvis and missing rainy days.

Jennifer Barton's fiction and nonfiction has appeared in numerous publications, such as *Hawk and Handsaw, Motif, Pindeldyboz, Lost, New Southerner,* and *Work,* and has been nominated for a Pushcart Prize. She received her MFA from the New School in New York City in 2007, and is currently a writing tutor in Knoxville, Tennessee.

Essayist, novelist, and poet **Wendell Berry** has written more than thirty books. He lives and works in his native Kentucky with his wife, Tanya Berry, and their children and grandchildren.

Tina Mozelle Braziel, a recent graduate of the University of Oregon MFA program, directs the Ada Long Creative Writing Workshop at the University of Alabama at Birmingham. Her poems have appeared or are forthcoming in *The Cincinnati Review, Poetry South, Birmingham Poetry Review,* and *Main Street Rag,* among other journals. She and her husband, novelist James Braziel, live and write in a glass cabin that they are building on Hydrangea Ridge.

Kathryn Cody is a freelance writer living in Lexington, Kentucky. Her work has been published in *The Peralta Press, The Listening Eye, Urban Spaghetti, Inscape Magazine, The Pacific Review, Blood & Thunder, Mentress Moon,* and other literary journals. She received honorable mention in the Best of Ohio Writers competition, and her latest endeavor is a creative nonfiction work in progress.

Jen Coleman has recently been a finalist for The Poetry Foundation's Ruth Lilly Poetry Fellowships and the Zone 3 Press First Book Award. Her work has appeared in *Buddhist Poetry Review, Fifth Wednesday Journal, New Welsh Review, The Southeast Review,* and elsewhere. She earned her MFA from Hollins University and currently teaches English at Dabney S. Lancaster Community College and Lynchburg College. She lives in Roanoke, Virginia with her two Manx cats.

Katherine Scott Crawford is an award-winning writer, newspaper columnist, and college English teacher. Author of the historical novel *Keowee Valley,* her work has appeared in literary journals and magazines, including *South Loop Review, The Santa Fe Writer's Project,* and *Wilderness House Literary Review.* Crawford holds an MFA in Creative Writing from Vermont College of Fine Arts and lives in Western North Carolina with her husband and daughters.

Richard Hague's prose has appeared in his collections *Milltown Natural: Essays & Stories From a Life*; *Learning How: Stories, Yarns, & Tales*; and *Lives of the Poem: Community & Connection in a Writing Life,* as well as in *Creative Nonfiction, Appalachian Journal, Now & Then, Pine Mountain Sand & Gravel,* and several anthologies. He received the 2012 Weatherford Award in Poetry. He lives, writes, and operates a small urban farm in Cincinnati.

Matthew Haughton is the author of *Stand in the Stillness of Woods* (WordTech Editions). His chapbook, *Bee-coursing Box* (Accents Publications) was nominated for the Weatherford Award for Appalachian Poetry. His poems have appeared in several publications including *Appalachian Journal, Now & Then, Still, Border Crossing,* and *The Louisville Review.* Haughton works as a public school teacher in his native Kentucky.

Melanie K. Hutsell lives in the foothills of the Smoky Mountains. Her short fiction has appeared in *Still: The Journal, Trajectory,* and the Knoxville Writers' Guild anthology *Outscape: Writings on Fences and Frontiers.* Very special thanks go to Cheri Frost Brown for the opportunity to experience a day in the life of a Smoky Mountain hotelkeeper, to the curators of the Little River Railroad and Lumber Company Museum, and to the members of her writing group.

Erin Keane is the author of three collections of poetry. Her latest, *Demolition of the Promised Land,* was published by Typecast Publishing in 2014. A recipient of the Al Smith Fellowship from the Kentucky Arts Council and a 2014 Fellow at the Eugene O'Neill Theater Center's National Critics Institute, Keane covers culture and entertainment for Salon.com.

Cathy Lentes's work has appeared in *Appalachian Heritage, Now & Then, Riverwind, Blueline,* and many other journals and anthologies. She received her MFA in Creative Writing from the Solstice Program of Pine Manor College in 2013.

Clarissa Nemeth is originally from Gatlinburg, Tennessee. She has a Bachelor of Music degree from Boston University, an MFA from North Carolina State University, and is currently a doctoral candidate in creative writing at the University of Kansas. She is working on a novel about the tourist towns of Sevier County, Tennessee. She lives in Lawrence, Kansas with her husband Greg and their pit bull, Boogie. Her work has also been featured in *The Writing Disorder.*

Adam Padgett's fiction has appeared in *Appalachian Heritage, Roanoke Review, Cold Mountain Review, SmokeLong Quarterly,* and reprinted in *Surreal South '13: An Anthology of Short Fiction.* He is a mentor for PEN America's Prison Writing Program and has been nominated for a Pushcart Prize.

Elaine Fowler Palencia, now of Champaign, Illinois, grew up in Morehead, Kentucky. She is the author of two poetry chapbooks and two collections of Appalachian short stories, *Small Caucasian Woman* and *Brier Country.* "Luck of the Draw" is included in her third collection, *Riding the Devil's Bicycle,* which is seeking a publisher. She is now at work on *My Dear Companion: The Civil War Letters of John M. Douthit.*

Savannah Sipple is a poet from Beattyville, Kentucky. Her work has been published in *Still: The Journal, Now & Then, Deep South Magazine, The Louisville Review, Appalachian Heritage, New Southerner,* and is forthcoming in *Southern Indiana Review.*

Nicholas Smith is an editor at *Wind: A Journal of Writing & Community.* A poet, he grew up in Knox County, Kentucky, and is a frequent contributor to *Still: The Journal.*

Terrell Jamal Terry's poems have appeared or are forthcoming in *Columbia Poetry Review, West Branch, Green Mountains Review, Washington Square, Interim,* and elsewhere. He resides in Raleigh, North Carolina.

Allison Thorpe recently retired from teaching literature, creative writing, and women's studies. She is the author of *Thoughts While Swinging a Wild Child in a Green Mesh Hammock, Swooning and Other Art Forms* (a NFSPS chapbook winner), *What She Sees: Poems for Georgia O'Keefe* (forthcoming from White Knuckle Press), and *To This Sad and Lovely Land*. A Pushcart nominee, she is currently working on her first novel.

Amanda Rachelle Warren is a displaced Appalachian whose poems have appeared in *Beloit Poetry Journal, Crazyhorse, Indiana Review, Pacific Review, Cimarron Review,* and *Hayden's Ferry Review*. She is the author of the chapbook *Ritual no.3: For the Exorcism of Ghosts,* a graduate of Western Michigan University's doctoral program in English, a former poetry editor for *Third Coast,* and currently works as an instructor at Georgia Regents University.

C. Williams's fiction has appeared in *The Louisville Review* and *Appalachian Heritage*. When not writing, she works as a production designer for sets in film, television, and commercials. She lives on the eastside of Nashville, Tennessee, the best neighborhood in the known world.

William Kelley Woolfitt is the author of two books of poetry, *Beauty Strip* (Texas Review Press, 2014) and *Charles of the Desert* (Paraclete Press, 2015). He teaches creative writing and literature at Lee University in Cleveland, Tennessee.